Praise for *Profit and the Practice of Law*

"What makes this book a must-read is Mike's keen perception of the current status of the profession and its attendant problems, as well as what may lie ahead for it without the changes he advocates. . . . All who value the profession would do well to study this book."

The Honorable Griffin B. Bell
Former Attorney General of the Uni
Judge, United States Fifth Circuit C
Partner, King & Spalding

"Michael Trotter's book *Profit and the Practice of Law* is a very important book and should be widely read. It is extremely entertaining and readable and the more compelling for that. It should be read by American lawyers because it articulates what many are prepared to say privately about private law practice . . . . The Book should be read with great care in Europe . . . . It should be read and talked about by lawyers throughout the United States and abroad - 'private practice reform thyself."

His Honor Judge John Toulmin CMG QC FKC,
Past President of the European Bar Council (CCBE), and Chairman of the Board of Trustees of the European Law Academy (ERA) 1997-2010, now Honorary Chairman for Life

"This book is both enjoyable and insightful. Michaèl Trotter can not only write well, but he has something to say. Thought and reflection are provoked on every page. Journalists, consultants, and numerous other outsiders have had a lot to say about law firms and law firm management. At last an insider, a reflective practitioner, gives us the inside view."

David H. Maister
Author of *Managing the Professional Service Firm* and *True Professionalism*, and a leading professional service firm consultant

"Mike Trotter has captured the essence of the evolution of major law firms in Atlanta (and around the country) from relatively small firms of lawyers who took professional pride in the quality of their work and in their roles as community leaders, to the very large law firms of today in which 'rainmakers' leverage the billable hours of associates to generate much larger profits than were ever dreamed of by their predecessors. In the process he very accurately describes the stress, fears, frustrations and ultimate dissatisfaction of many of the lawyers practicing in this system, as well as the rise of in-house law departments, all with a generous serving of historical facts related not only to law firm economics, but to the lifestyles of lawyers."

Robert S. Harkey
Retired Senior Vice President - General Counsel and Secretary
Delta Air Lines, Inc.

"Trotter is unusual in that he has taken time out from the drudgery of racking up billable hours to reflect on what is happening to the legal profession and what that means for the profession and society. . . . Everything that he says about the changes in the practice of law in the United States, we too have seen in Britain. . . . Trotter explains how the single-minded pursuit of profit has a tremendous knock on effect. It reaches deep into the ways in which law is practiced and the way the public perceives the profession. The effects are not just cosmetic but have profound consequences for access to justice, maintenance of professional standards, and the self-esteem of lawyers. This book is strongly commended to all lawyers and is readily accessible to the lay reader."

Julian P. Killingley
Professor of Law
Birmingham City University School of Law
Birmingham, England

"I think your book is the best analysis of what I know of the state of legal practice today and how it came about, and I am sending copies to everyone I think should read it."

Louis J. Hector
Former Senior Partner
Steel Hector & Davis
Miami, Florida

"I just finished your book, and I couldn't wait to tell you what a masterful job you've done. I rarely use the word "brilliant". . . but I can't think of a better way to describe your outstanding combination of scholarship and insight. Based on my own experience, I agree with every single one of your points. . . . What impressed me most was that, while I wasn't at all surprised by any of the factual data, I found the conclusions you drew from them nothing short of astounding. You have literally provided me with a structure for what were, until now, my noncohesive attitudes and beliefs about our profession and my own career."

Jerold Zieselman
Retired Partner
Proskauer Rose LLP,
New York

"Mike Trotter deftly combines scholarship, legal analysis and serious journalism to provide a candid and lively insider's view of how the law business has evolved over the past several decades. I learned a great deal from this revealing book and highly recommend it to anyone interested in the economics and mores of law firms and lawyers."

Paul M. Barrett
Assistant Managing Editor
Bloomberg Businessweek, and author of
GLOCK: The Rise of America's Gun (Crown),
among other books

"This is a wonderful book . . . . It is written with great clarity, a 'must read' for all lawyers and law students, as well as vital for others. Trotter lucidly explains the unhappiness of the public with lawyers, and lawyers' unhappiness with lawyering."

Alan Watson
Ernest P. Rogers Professor of Law
University of Georgia School of Law

"I have read your book from cover to cover, and found it engrossing. Your book chronicles graphically the transition from law partnership to 'big law service business' that has occurred in many firms that I know. It is a Must Read for lawyers in big firms and firms that want to become big firms, and, of course, in-house general counsels interested in obtaining quality legal services at reasonable cost. I would be surprised if the book is not required reading soon for first year law students across the country."

John H. Cutler
Retired Partner
Heller Ehrman
San Francisco

"*Profit and the Practice of Law* written by Michael Trotter is an extremely interesting and mentally challenging book."

Chesterfield Smith
Former Senior Partner and Founder of Holland & Knight, and Former President of the American Bar Association

"Mike Trotter truthfully describes the changes, often negative, that have occurred in the private practice of law during the past twenty years and wisely suggests that lawyers chart a different course for the future. I highly recommend this book to all who are interested in the legal profession."

Nancy L. Henry
Former Senior Vice President and Chief Legal Counsel
The Dun & Bradstreet Corporation

"This book is well written and easy to read. . . . A must read for any lawyer seriously interested in the future of the profession."

Hazel L. Johnson
Former Editor of "Resources and Reviews" in
Law Practice Management
Published by the Law Practice Management Section of the American Bar Association

"*Profit and the Practice of Law* makes a strong contribution to the literature on contemporary law practice and, as a kind of autobiography, to our understanding of the history of the bar since World War II. . . . What I like most about this manuscript is the sure touch that the author has for his subject. He knows the practice of law, the world of Atlanta's business community, and the ways in which major business law firms operate. He also has a fine sense of the relationship of legal education to the major firms, the role played by the cost allocation and profit-center models that propel most firms, the impact of technology and 'economic opportunity' on the shape of the firms, and the impact of 'modern' legal accounting practices on the ways in which lawyers charge for their services and relate to one another. Indeed, in this regard, the book is something of a triumph."

Kermit L. Hall
Former Dean and Professor of History and Law
College of Humanities
Ohio State University

"I believe you did a splendid job of articulating what has come of the legal profession in the context of "major business practice firms," as you call them, in the time since you and I left Harvard Law School. All applicants to law schools today should have to certify that they have read this book (and understand it) before their applications will be processed."

John C. Christie, Jr.
Retired Partner
WilmerHale
Washington, D.C.

"Trotter's book is a poignant tale of the rise and fall of the corporate law firm told from the heart by one who has lived through its transformation. Trotter traces the economic and legal trends that have made law and lawyering unnecessarily expensive and often non-productive. . . . The book serves as a compelling wake-up call to corporate clients to once again take control of their legal destinies by refusing to abide by the prevailing practices of the typical "big firm" lawyer."

Thomas B. Metzloff
Professor of Law
Duke University School of Law

"It seems to me a very important book for everybody in your profession, whether they are only thinking of studying law, are about to graduate from law school, or are now practicing. . . . Congratulations on a brilliant accomplishment!"

Roderick F. O'Connor
Professor of Management Emeritus
Georgia Institute of Technology

"[Y]ou've done an outstanding job in the study of the legal profession during the period of time that you and I have been in practice . . . . Congratulations on a job well done."

Elliot Goldstein
Former Senior Partner
Powell, Goldstein, Frazer & Murphy LLP
Atlanta. Georgia

"Mr. Trotter has done a great job of describing how the practice of law has changed over the past four decades. . . . Most members of the Bar will find this book interesting reading no matter how long they have been in practice. The changes which have occurred in the legal profession, as well as in the practice of law, are set forth in a clear and concise manner with supporting facts and figures. The book explains not only how these changes have occurred, but also why. . . . This book should also be of interest to non-lawyers. . . . Whether the readers agree or disagree with the author's views about changes in the practice of law, it is certain that they will find this book informative. Moreover, it should be required reading for first-year law students."

The Honorable Robert W. Chasteen, Jr.
Judge of the Superior Court for Cordele Judicial Circuit and Former President of the State Bar of Georgia

"I am writing to let you know what great pleasure I derive from knowing that I will be able to return home at the end of the day and read another dozen pages of your 1997 book. It's GREAT! I find it so intellectually keen and revealing on a subject I thought I knew all about that I have been motivated to let you know. I have taught a course at Nova Law Center in Fort Lauderdale, Florida, for almost 30 years in the history of the American legal profession and yet never managed to learn anything interesting about the transformation of not just the large, business firm but, really, the way the whole idea of being a lawyer is different now than it was back when I decided to go to
law school."

Anthony Chase
Author of *Law and History: The Evolution of the American Legal System*

"Recently I have read your book *Profit and the Practice of Law*, which I found interested me very much. I guess some lawyers from many other countries are also having the same experiences described in your book. . . . Although the early period of the legal business described in your book was 30 to 35 years ago, it nevertheless matched my experiences of the 1980s when I was just starting my own practice. But those descriptions about in-house lawyers, computer-oriented documentation, rude attitude of the US lawyers, bankruptcy of clients and poor productivity of the young lawyers in the major firms can be seen more and more in our daily work here, too."

Mark M Koen
Koen and Koen
Taipei, Taiwan

Profit
and the
Practice
of Law

WHAT'S HAPPENED TO

THE LEGAL PROFESSION

Michael H. Trotter

Michael H. Trotter received his law degree from the Harvard Law School in 1962, and his B.A, degree from Brown University *cum laude* (Phi Beta Kappa) in 1958. He then entered the Harvard University Ph.D. Program in American History as a Woodrow Wilson Fellow and was awarded a Master's Degree in History in 1959. While practicing as a partner in two Am Law 100 firms and three entrepreneurial law firms, he has been a keen student of the economics and ethos of modern law practice, as well as an occasional columnist for Atlanta's legal newspaper, *The Daily Report.* He has written widely on issues of law firm management, operations and economics, and has taught related courses, as well as courses in securities regulation, at the Emory University School of Law. He is also the author of *Pig in a Poke? The Uncertain Advantages of Very Large and Highly Leveraged Law Firms in America*, which appeared as a chapter in the American Bar Association's publication, *Raise the Bar – Real World Solutions for a Troubled Profession (2007).* His latest book on the major business practice law firms, *Declining Prospects: How Extraordinary Competition and Compensation Are Changing America's Major Law Firms,* will be published in early 2012. He is a partner in the Atlanta law firm of Taylor English Duma LLP.

Profit and the Practice of Law was first published in 1997 and was well received by practicing lawyers and students of the legal profession alike. The book has emerged as the definitive work on growth and change in the major business practice law firms in America between 1960 and 1995. It is now clear that the trends we had experienced in the United States were also occurring in other countries as widely diverse as the United Kingdom and Taiwan.

In recent years I've been asked to set in print my thoughts on developments in the legal profession since 1995. Ed Bean, the Editor in Chief of *The Daily Report*, in particular urged me to do so. The resulting book, *Declining Prospects: How Extraordinary Competition and Compensation Are Changing America's Major Law Firms* will be available in early 2012.

In *Declining Prospects* I have not undertaken to repeat all of the history set forth in *Profit and the Practice of Law*. The two books together are intended to be a consolidated history of growth and change in the major business practice firms in America from the early fifties through 2010. It is not possible to understand how the legal profession, and in particular how the major business practice firms, have gotten to where they are today without understanding from whence they came.

Chapters Five through Twelve of *Profit and the Practice of Law* address some of the problems of the major law firms and the legal system in America. Unfortunately most of the problems noted in 1997 are still with us today, and some are worse than in earlier times. The remedies suggested here still offer some hope of reformation.

I remain grateful to my family, friends and professional colleagues who encouraged me to write *Profit and the Practice of Law* and whose support and assistance made it possible.

TO SUE

CONTENTS

PREFACE

his book has its origins in a career-long interest in why lawyers do what they do and, more particularly, in a speech I gave to the corporate counsel section of the State Bar of Georgia in February 1990 on changes in the practice of corporate law in Atlanta, Georgia, since 1960. The extraordinary level of interest and comment that was generated by the speech led me to increase my research and to participate in panel discussions on the subject. The speech was published in its entirety on March 5, 1990, in the *Fulton County Daily Report*, an Atlanta area affiliate of the *American Lawyer*, and I was surprised to receive calls from around the country from lawyers who had seen a copy of the text. One California lawyer called to ask for a copy because he was having difficulty reading a worn copy of the article that the general counsel for one of his New York clients had given him with the admonition that he should read it. In 1993 I became an adjunct professor at the Emory University School of Law and a research fellow, teaching a seminar in "Legal Service Delivery and Law Practice Economics" and a course in "The Transformation of the Practice of Law."

I began my legal studies at the Harvard Law School in the fall of 1959 and spent the summer of 1960 as a summer clerk at the Atlanta firm of Alston, Sibley, Miller, Spann & Shackelford. I returned to the Alston firm[1] for a second summer in 1961 and joined the firm as an associate in the summer of 1962. I became a partner in the fall of 1967 and served at various times as chairman of the firm's corporate department, chairman of the recruiting committee, and chairman of the facilities committee. The Alston firm is now the sixty-ninth largest law firm in America.[2]

In 1970 I became the firm's attorney primarily responsible for the work of Citizens and Southern Realty Investors (the "Trust"), a real estate investment trust ("REIT") sponsored and managed by the Citizens and Southern National Bank, the Alston firm's largest and most important client and then the largest bank in the southeastern United States.[3] In 1971 I became a trustee of the Trust (the equivalent of a director), a position I held for ten years. Within four years C&S Realty was the fifth largest REIT in the country and, perhaps because the Trust experienced serious difficulties as a result of the real estate recession of the midseventies, it had become the Alston firm's second largest fee-paying client.

In 1974, it came to my attention that the C&S National Bank, as manager of the Trust, had on occasion invested the Trust's funds to its disadvantage in transactions that differed from those approved by the Trustees and, in a number of instances, had an undisclosed interest in transactions financed by the Trust. As a result, the Trust had significant claims against the bank, and I found myself in the middle of this dispute between my firm's two largest clients. After wrestling with the problem for almost three years, I resigned as a partner in the firm, primarily to resolve the conflict and to protect the interests of the firm in its relationship with its largest client.

I played a major role in organizing a new firm under the name Trotter, Bondurant, Griffin, Miller & Hishon and remained with that firm for five years. In 1982 the *American Lawyer* identified the firm as Atlanta's "New Powerhouse," and my picture appeared on the cover of that issue with my partner, Emmet Bondurant.[4] Differences among some of the partners (not including Mr. Bondurant) caused me and five of my closest working colleagues to leave that firm in November 1982 to organize a new firm named Trotter Smith & Jacobs. During the 1980s, Trotter Smith became the thirteenth largest law firm in Atlanta with sixty-five lawyers at its peak.

The bankruptcy of the firm's two largest clients, accounting for approximately 70 percent of its business, in the midst of a recession proved to be an insurmountable obstacle to the firm's survival, and we elected to close its operations as of February 28, 1992. The firm had almost fifty lawyers at the time of its closing. I am now a partner in Kilpatrick & Cody, the 138th largest law firm in the United States and one of Atlanta's oldest and largest firms with over two hundred lawyers and offices in Atlanta and Augusta, Georgia, Washington, D.C., London, and Brussels.

I have had experience both as a lawyer with two big corporate firms and as an entrepreneurial lawyer, having served as managing partner of sizable and growing law firms for almost fifteen years. Both Trotter, Bondurant and Trotter Smith & Jacobs were listed during most of their respective existences in the *Martindale-Hubbell Bar Register of Preeminent Lawyers*, an exclusive listing of corporate law firms in the United States. My articles on law firm management issues have appeared in the *American Bar Association Journal*, the *National Law Journal* and the *Georgia Journal of Southern Legal History*.[5]

It would not have been possible to write this story by relying on publicly available information alone. Most of the important financial and operating data reflected on these pages has never been published and could be obtained only from firms that had preserved their records from the 1960s and 1970s and from interviews with lawyers who practiced law during those years.

Fortunately, I kept a good deal of information about my own practice and my various firms including my daily time records from my first day on the job at the Alston firm. When it became known in Atlanta that I was writing this book, some friends began offering me information about their own practices and their firms. In addition, I appealed to the managing partners of several of the large Atlanta firms and sought their cooperation. Some responded enthusiastically and as fully as their records would permit. Some had not maintained records from the 1960s, and others did not want to invest the time and effort necessary to find the information. Those who did cooperate were not willing to make information available if it would be linked to them or their law firms. As a result, much of the information I have developed has come to me on the express condition that it not be used in a way that would divulge the identity of the firm supplying it.

With the information available in the burgeoning legal press, combined with the information I had and was able to develop on a private basis, I was able to write this book. I then distributed a draft to prominent Atlanta lawyers (both house counsel and private practitioners) and asked them to review the book for historical accuracy and analytical soundness. In particular I asked them to verify the information about billing rates and lawyer compensation. Their responses confirmed or expanded my information and reassured me of the accuracy of the factual data and of my analysis of the process of transformation in the profession.

I am grateful to Dean Howard O. Hunter and the Emory University School of Law for giving me the opportunity to teach courses on the subject matter of this book. I could not have completed this project without the able assistance of David Eaton, a student at the law school and executive managing editor of the *Emory Law Journal*, who worked with me as a research and editorial assistant. I am indebted to several friends who read and commented on the text including Lloyd Whitaker, Miles Alexander,

Wayne Shortridge, Paul Bellows, Neil Williams, James Sibley, Elliott Goldstein, Bradley Hale, James Steinberg, and Neil Falis. I am most indebted to my wife, Sue Sexton Trotter, for her editing of the text.

INTRODUCTION

The years 1960 to 1995 witnessed the transformation of corporate law firms in America from small, dignified, prosperous, conservative, white male professional partnerships dedicated to serving their clients and communities into large, aggressive, wealthy, self-promoting, diverse business organizations where money is often valued more highly than service to clients or community. During this period, the number of lawyers in the United States grew from approximately 286,000 in 1962 to an estimated 930,000 in 1995.[1]

The largest law firm in America in 1960 was Shearman, Sterling & Wright of New York City, which had 125 lawyers. By 1995 Jones, Day, Reavis & Pogue had 1,053 lawyers practicing in the

United States and an annual gross revenue for 1994 of $384 million. Close behind in size was Skadden, Arps, Slate, Meagher & Flom with 1,042 lawyers working in the United States but with the greatest gross revenues of any American firm in 1994: $582 million. In the same year, average profits per partner in the most profitable business practice firm in the country, the 57-partner firm of Wachtell, Lipton, Rosen & Katz of New York City, reached $1.4 million.[2]

This book concerns itself with lawyers and firms delivering legal services to major business clients. These lawyers have long been viewed as the elite of the profession. Their representation of the largest and most powerful businesses in America and the world carries great power, prestige, and economic rewards. The story focuses on the eight largest and most influential firms in Atlanta, Georgia, that existed in 1960 and have survived to this day as major firms, though two merged in the early sixties and the resulting firm has now become the Atlanta office of a national firm headquartered elsewhere. These eight firms are representative of the many large business practice firms located in major cities around the United States, and the transformation they have undergone mirrors to a significant degree what has occurred in the profession nationwide.

The growth in number and size of large business practice firms has resulted in part from the growth in significance of law in our society during the past thirty-five years. Legal issues in business have become pervasive. Business clients who once needed a lawyer only occasionally now need one or more all day, every day. As a response to the growing pervasiveness of legal issues and spiraling legal costs, businesses have hired lawyers to work for them full time "in-house" as employees. The in-house revolution is one of the major changes involved in the dramatic restructuring of the legal profession.

Clients have become increasingly dissatisfied as they have seen their legal costs soar. Costs have risen because of the inexorable growth in complexity of business relationships and agreements;

the growth in legislation at all governmental levels creating new legal rights and more government regulation; the more frequent use of law and litigation by private parties to regulate their affairs; changes in the way law is practiced that have increased the lawyer time spent on legal transactions; and higher fees charged by law firms for such time. The accelerating growth of the legal profession since 1960, which began as a practical response to the growing demand for legal services, turned into a "plantation system" in which the increasing number and proportion of associates generated growing profits for the partners, while the partners created a smaller proportion of the firms' profits from their own labors. Together, these factors have raised the cost of legal services substantially in excess of the rate of inflation.

Although New York City remains the home of more of the largest and most profitable business practice firms than any other city (27 of the 100 largest, 9 of the top 10 and 31 of the top 100 in profits per partner), all such firms that have survived in the United States, including those in New York, have grown and changed in similar ways, and regional differences have largely disappeared. Of the twenty-five largest firms headquartered in the United States, six are headquartered in New York and six in Chicago. Of the top ten in size, only two are headquartered in New York, with three in Chicago and two in Los Angeles. However, of the top twenty-five firms, only three do not have a sizable office in New York City where a substantial number of the largest transactions are still handled.

By the 1990s, business lawyers were earning much more money in real dollars, and most were working harder than they had in 1960. At the same time many lawyers have grown increasingly dissatisfied with their work and with their lives, and the reputation of the profession as a whole has suffered a steady decline. It is ironic that the growth in the size of business practice firms and the increased compensation of their lawyers has been accompanied by such rising dissatisfaction and declining status. These changes are evidenced by the many books that have been written on these subjects. Recent books addressing some of these issues include Deborah L. Arron's *Running from the Law*, Richard D. Kahlenberg's *Broken Contract*, and Richard W. Moll's *Lure of the Law*.[3] Seminars are also widely offered to aid the disaffected in the search for new careers. A recent example is a seminar in February 1994 given at Georgetown University in Washington, called "J.D. Preferred: 400+ Things You Can Do with a Law Degree (Other Than Practice Law)."

There are increasingly frequent expressions of concern by the organized legal profession about the decline of "professionalism" in the legal establishment. The American Bar Association and many of the state bar associations have sponsored studies and meetings to discuss this loss and to find ways to repair the profession.[4] Many states now require practicing lawyers to take periodic courses in "professionalism" in order to retain their licenses to practice law. Most of these efforts are based on the premise that along the way lawyers made conscious decisions to alter their patterns of conduct and that a reform effort can bring the profession back to older and higher standards. Other examples of these concerns are found in *The Betrayed Profession* by Sol Linowitz, the former outside general counsel of Xerox, and *The Lost Lawyer* by Anthony T. Kronman, the new dean of the Yale Law School.[5]

These efforts to revive the lost and lamented professionalism of the bar are doomed to failure, because the changes in lawyers' behavior result from fundamental changes in the economics, structure, and functioning of the profession and changes in the business world to which it relates. Conditions cannot be put back the way they were. Without first understanding the profound changes that have occurred, there can be no successful effort to reform how lawyers behave in this altered environment, nor can most lawyers regain control over their own lives. Lawyers have behaved as normal human beings responding to the circumstances in which they have found themselves, circumstances that have evolved over the past thirty-five years. Lawyers are not the only ones who have been affected. The change has been felt throughout the entire international business community.

The book describes the transformation that has occurred in the legal profession and in the practice of law, and it explains why and how it has come about. It also proposes reforms in how legal services are delivered to clients by business practice firms, as well as reforms in the legal system itself with a view toward improving the quality of legal services while reducing costs.

Profit
& the
Practice
of Law

1 The Practice of Law in 1960

In 1960, the largest law firm in Atlanta serving major business clients, Crenshaw, Hansell, Ware, Brandon & Dorsey, had twenty-one lawyers.[1] The seven other elite firms in Atlanta each had fewer than twenty lawyers. They were Smith, Kilpatrick, Cody, Rogers & McClatchey (sixteen lawyers); Alston, Sibley, Miller, Spann & Shackelford (fifteen); Spalding, Sibley, Troutman, Meadow & Smith (fifteen); Powell, Goldstein, Frazer & Murphy (thirteen); Sutherland, Asbill & Brennan (twenty but eight were located in the Washington, D.C., office); Troutman, Sams, Schroder & Lockerman (ten); and Moise, Post & Gardner (nine). In 1960, the largest firm in America, Shearman, Sterling & Wright of New York City, had 125 lawyers.[2]

The partners providing leadership in the major Atlanta firms as they began to grow rapidly in the late 1960s and early 1970s were men in their late fifties and early sixties who had spent their entire professional lives in what we would consider today to be very small law firms. Most of these men were legal generalists and practiced law competently across several practice areas. Law firm management issues had been relatively uncomplicated for them, and they were not prepared for the extraordinary growth of their firms as it started to happen. They did not have the time to analyze what was going on or to develop their management skills as growth continued. Over the "boom" years they were too busy scrambling to provide legal services to their expanding clientele and trying to supervise their growing number of associates to either look very far into the future or to ponder the past. If they had looked back, they might have been shocked by how much and how fast their professional world had changed.

FIRM SIZE

In 1960 the law firms serving the needs of major business clients were much smaller than they are today. As already noted, the largest firm in Atlanta in 1960 had twenty-one lawyers. The next largest firm had sixteen.[3] There were twelve firms with ten or more lawyers in Atlanta at that time. A firm that every corporate lawyer in Atlanta would have considered a major firm, Moise, Post & Gardner, which merged with the Hansell firm in 1962, had nine lawyers. All major firms in Atlanta were small by current standards.

The larger firms in the country were mostly headquartered in New York where there were only three firms with more than 100 lawyers and none with over 125. There were seventeen firms outside New York that employed more than fifty attorneys in 1960.

SEASONED PROFESSIONALS

After their small size, the most striking feature of most of the
business practice law firms of 1960, when compared with 1996,
was the small number of associates in relationship to the number
of partners. The largest firm in Atlanta at that time, the Hansell
firm, had seventeen partners and four associates.[4] The Alston firm
and the Spalding firm each had ten partners and five associates.
Among the seven largest firms, only Smith, Kilpatrick, Cody,
Rogers & McClatchey (seven partners and nine associates) had
more associates than partners. Another firm in the top eight,
Troutman, Sams, Schroder & Lockerman, had eight partners and
two associates.[5]

Associates were usually young lawyers who came to work for
the firms out of law school (there were very few former judicial
clerks because there were few judges and some of them had per-
manent clerks) and worked for the firms for four to six years before being asked to become partners or to leave. As a general rule
most firms had an "up or out" policy, and therefore the only per-
manent associates were one or two holdovers from the prior
decades. A majority of the associates hired at Smith, Kilpatrick
in the 1950s and early 1960s became partners, and the percentage
of those making partner at the other major firms was generally
much higher.

SLOW GROWTH

Most of the major business practice law firms in Atlanta had
grown from six to ten lawyers in 1940 to ten to fifteen lawyers in
1960. The Alston firm had ten lawyers in 1940, both Powell, Goldstein and the Troutman firm had nine, and the Spalding firm had
seven. The firms generally lost ground during World War II as
lawyers entered the military service (at one point the Sutherland

firm had only two lawyers), and they grew very slowly during the late 1940s and the 1950s. Consequently, the number of jobs with these firms that were available to graduating law students in 1960 was very limited, and the firms generally had their choice of the cream of the student crop. New associates were hired to meet existing demand rather than in anticipation of additional business.

Prior to the 1960s, few of these firms hired more than one new associate per year or hired one in two consecutive years. There were, of course, differences among the firms. The Kilpatrick firm hired more lawyers during the 1950s than the other firms (in several years it hired two new associates), and fewer of its associates remained with the firm to become partners. The firms rarely sent recruiters to law schools to interview; the students were expected to come to the firms' offices in Atlanta to visit at their own expense. Given the pace at which the Georgia and the national economies were growing in the late 1950s and early 1960s, most firms could easily keep up with the growth in business by hiring a new associate every year or two.

The pace of hiring increased in the early sixties, but the partners were uncertain about future growth of demand for services and remained cautious. For example, the Alston firm hired four new associates in Atlanta in 1966 and six more in 1967 but hired only one new associate in 1968. Similarly, the Hansell firm probably felt it had hired excessively when it took on eight new associates in 1964; it hired only two in 1965.

HIGH STANDARDS

It was rare for one of these firms to hire a student who was not in the top quarter of his class at the Harvard or Yale law school, or who had not been an editor of the law journal at a highly regarded regional or local law school. Law schools made class standing information available to law firms in 1960 so that the firms could be certain they were hiring the top students. When I was offered a job at Sutherland, Asbill & Brennen in the winter of 1961, I was told that I was the first Harvard law student to whom they had offered a job who was not in the top 10 percent of his class.

During my first summer at the Alston firm, one of the younger partners who had graduated magna cum laude from the Harvard Law School asked me regularly if my grades had arrived. One night I dreamed that I had finished in the top quarter of the class, and I was pleased with the nocturnal report. The next time my inquisitor asked me about my grades I told him of my dream, because the real grades had not yet arrived. His response was that he hoped the dream did not prove to be correct because it would be a poor result. I experienced a number of uncomfortable days until the real grades appeared and my dream was proven to be correct. I was made to feel that I had gotten in the door of the firm by the skin of my teeth. Students were expected to have outstanding undergraduate records as well and to have achieved distinction in areas outside the classroom. In addition to being evaluated for their intellect and their grades, they were also scrutinized for their poise and social compatibility with the firm, and no married man was hired unless his spouse had also been looked over.

WORKING CONDITIONS AND BILLABLE HOURS

The practice of corporate law at the major business practice firms in Atlanta was a full-time occupation for those engaged in it in the early 1960s. Most of the lawyers worked routinely eight to nine hours a day, five days a week and half a day or more on Saturday. They worked longer hours at night, on weekends, and on holidays when their clients' needs required it. Many felt overworked, and their families complained that they never saw them at home or that they were always bringing work home with them.

The Kilpatrick firm had the reputation of being the hardest working place in town with a regular diet of night and weekend work. The story is told at the firm of a midnight call in 1964 from a senior superior court judge who was looking for a citation and who knew he was likely to find some help at the Kilpatrick firm even at that late hour, and he did.

The Alston firm was ahead of its time in maintaining billable and nonbillable time records in 1960 when I first arrived at the firm, and most of the firm's lawyers, including some of the senior partners, kept their records faithfully.

Those lawyers who recorded their time were not nearly as aggressive about recording it as billable time as lawyers are today. Many firms did not keep track of the amount of time invested in a client's projects until later in the sixties. Those that kept time did so as a point of reference in billing clients. Billing was based on a variety of considerations including the importance of the work, the results obtained, and the bar association's minimum fee schedules. Although some firms routinely required their individual lawyers to keep time records and this information was deposited in client time files where it could be retrieved in determining a client's bill, none of the firms kept track of the total billable time recorded by individual attorneys.

Although many lawyers in the early 1960s spent as much time at their offices as lawyers do now, those that recorded time did not record nearly as many billable hours as they do today. I know from my own records that I recorded approximately 1,300 hours of billable time at the Alston firm in 1964; and in 1995, because of a heavy civic load, about 1,100. My best guess is that my contemporaries at the Kilpatrick firm in the sixties were working at a rate that would have produced 2,000 or more billable hours by today's standards of timekeeping. Because time was not systematically recorded at most firms, it is difficult to know for sure.

Many partners under the age of sixty billed fewer than one thousand hours a year, and some only a few hundred. In fact, no one was counting. In the late 1960s, the Alston firm considered a recommendation of its long-range planning committee that each partner be required to bill at least eight hundred hours a year in the absence of a special dispensation. The recommendation was turned down by the management committee.

It is important not to confuse recorded billable hours with hours worked. A senior partner at the Kilpatrick firm remembers it being said in the late 1950s by one of his senior colleagues that a lawyer who spent all day at the office for an entire week would be lucky to have four hours of effort that could be billed to clients. Time spent at the courthouse waiting for a trial to begin or in general background research or nonproductive research were among the items deemed inappropriate for billing to clients even if the time were recorded, and it was not billed at most firms in the early 1960s.

BILLING RATES

It is difficult to compare charges for legal services in the early 1960s with today's charges, because records have not been kept in a way to facilitate such comparisons. Most Atlanta firms in the early 1960s did not charge their clients based on the amount of time invested in projects for them, and many of them did not systematically keep time records. Many clients paid retainers, which provided their law firms with a stable financial base. For instance, the Kilpatrick firm's income from retainers in the early 1960s was sufficient to pay all of the firm's operating expenses except partner compensation.

Most retainer arrangements were reviewed annually, and some permitted additional billing if the work performed included major matters that had not been contemplated at the beginning of the year. In many cases, if the work had been priced on an hourly rate basis the price would have greatly exceeded the retainer payment received. Later, when firms became accustomed to thinking in terms of billable hours, they became dissatisfied with most of their retainer arrangements because the hourly return was less than their normal hourly rates.

It is my best recollection, confirmed by my fellow associates of those days, that the hourly rate for a starting associate at the Alston firm in 1962 was $20 an hour. Although I have been told by one of my former senior partners that according to his recollection his hourly billing rate was $90 an hour in 1962, there is some evidence that such a rate would have been high. Although a ratio of approximately 3:1 between the highest lawyer rate and the lowest is not unusual today, a ratio of 4.5:1 in 1960 seems unusual and may not be correct.

In response to an article I prepared for the *American Bar Association Journal*,[6] Mary Ann Altman, one of the leading law firm consultants in the country, searched for evidence of partner billing rates in the early sixties. She concluded that senior partner rates in 1962 were nearer to $45 an hour than to $90. This conclusion was based on a slender reed of information. She found that a speaker at a Practicing Law Institute seminar in 1962 suggested that the appropriate billing rate for a senior partner should be $50 an hour, for a junior partner $35, and for associates $15 to $20. Based on my research, I believe that senior partner billing rates in Atlanta in 1962, for those firms that had them, were in the range of $60 to $90 an hour. I assume that the rates were significantly higher in New York City, just as they are today.

THE PRICE OF LEGAL SERVICES

Based on my personal records, here are some examples of charges for legal services between 1962 and 1964: $60 for an individual bankruptcy; $100 to probate or draft a simple will; $250 for a court appearance to challenge the service of legal process; $450 to organize a simple corporation; $6,000 to $10,000 for representation of an issuer in an underwritten public offering of securities; $150 to amend a corporate charter; $1,100 for the sale of a chemical business; $2,500 to $3,000 to represent a large New York–based underwriter in a private placement of utility bonds with institutional investors; $2,400 to represent an issuer in the private placement of $1 million of debentures; and $2,250 for the reorganization of a leasing company. These charges can be compared with those today by applying a factor of five to reflect the approximately 400 percent inflation since that time. It is obvious that the cost of most such projects today is much more than the inflation-adjusted price.

ASSOCIATE COMPENSATION

As a result of the competition for their jobs, the firms did not have to pay much money to attract top talent. Several Atlanta firms did not seek students from the national law schools and had no need to worry about pay scales in other cities. Some firms were not accustomed to being asked what they paid and thought it was inappropriate for an applicant to raise the question. An offer on any terms was good enough. The major firms in Atlanta could employ top students for $300 a month: $3,600 a year in 1960. (The Alston firm paid $275 a month if the new associate were single and $300 if he were married.) The Kilpatrick firm paid a substantial premium of $100 a month over the other firms in the late 1950s, but settled for the going rate around 1962. In 1960, summer clerks (law students hired for the summer) were paid $200 a month. The starting salary in 1940 of some of these Atlanta firms had been $25 a week. For twenty years there had not been much pressure or need to change. What was true in Atlanta was also true in the rest of the country during this era. Despite major differences in the cost of living, the nation's most prominent law firms headquartered in New York paid starting salaries in 1960 of $500 a month, or $6,000 a year.

Many of the firms' senior partners had come from families that were able to assist them during their early years in practice. Without such assistance it was difficult for a young associate to make ends meet, especially if he had a spouse who did not work outside the home (in 1960 many wives were in this category). Without a supplemental source of income, or at least an aunt with a vacant basement apartment, one had to be prepared to make financial sacrifices to enter the practice of law. One of my friends, when he was hired at Spalding, Sibley, Troutman, Meadow & Smith in 1961, remembers being told by Griffin Bell that he would be paid $400 a month but that he would be unable to live on it.

The fact that associates were not well paid at first, and indeed would have to wait quite a while before realizing any substantial economic benefit from practicing law, was a deterrent that kept the supply of young lawyers low. (In the 1962 – 63 academic year, there were fewer than 50,000 students enrolled in law school, and only 9,638 students graduated from law schools that year.) No one entered the profession expecting to be immediately prosperous. I remember well my first day at the Alston firm as a summer associate in 1960. I shared the small library as an office with a starting associate who wore shirts with frayed collars and cuffs and holes in the sleeves. His suit was an outdated model he had purchased in high school. He felt lucky to be there, though, and would not have dreamed of complaining about his compensation of $275 a month. When I started as an associate in 1962, I owned a 1949 Chevrolet with over 100,000 miles on the odometer, and my wife and I lived in a small apartment that a widowed woman had made in her home. We paid $85 a month in rent (the equivalent of about $425 today) and were thrilled with my job and our good fortune. We were prepared to wait for economic reward. I remember an evening we spent with friends in the midsixties when the conversation turned to the question of how much one would have to earn per year to be "rich." The sum we agreed on was $25,000. I am told that had a similar group gathered in the late 1950s, $10,000 a year would have been the answer.

PARTNER COMPENSATION

The law firms that provided legal services to the leading businesses in their areas were stable and prosperous organizations in 1960. The partners in such firms were well paid for their efforts, but few became rich men from their legal practices alone. Several of Atlanta's major firms have made information available to me about their partner compensation during the early 1960s. The compensation paid to first-year partners at most firms was approximately $20,000, and one firm apparently paid about $41,000. These figures, adjusted for inflation, would be comparable to about $100,000 to $205,000 today.

Senior partner compensation is more difficult to compare. At least some senior partners served as trustees of substantial trusts set up by clients in earlier years, and in this capacity some received significant income that did not flow through the firm. In addition, some senior partners served as officers or directors of corporations and received salaries for doing so. Although the salary and director fee income usually, but not always, went to the firm, the partner might also benefit from participating in the client's pension and profit-sharing plans.

In any event, the direct cash compensation to the most highly compensated partners in Atlanta in 1960 ranged from approximately $45,000 at the low end to approximately $93,000 at the high end. The one senior partner earning $93,000 had an unusually good year. The next highest paid senior partner in the city earned about $85,000. Adjusted for inflation, these incomes would be comparable to earning about $225,000 to $425,000 in 1995. The ratio of compensation of the highest paid partner to the beginning partner's compensation was a bit more than 2:1, and the ratio of the highest paid partner's compensation to the starting associate's salary was as high as 26:1. Some of the major firms were much more profitable than others. Although the lawyers liked to speculate about their relative performance, it was not deemed appropriate to share such information, so no one knew for sure.

CLIENT RELATIONSHIPS

In 1960, law firms had their clients, and most had had them for a long time. At the Alston firm, which had been founded in 1893, many of the firm's major clients in 1960 had become clients before any of the existing partners had begun practicing law. The same was true at most of the other established firms. For this reason, among others, the clients were usually viewed as assets of the firm rather than as belonging to individual lawyers. In addition, because most clients did not have in-house lawyers, the firms did all of the clients' legal work, and usually several of the firm's lawyers were involved. Each of the large banks in Atlanta was represented by one or more of the major firms, but not all of the major firms represented a large bank. Most of the major businesses headquartered in Atlanta were also represented by one of the large firms, and each firm served as local, state, or regional counsel to national companies headquartered elsewhere.

Thirty years ago it was not uncommon for a senior lawyer to devote most of his time to one major client, functioning in the role of general legal counselor and adviser. Often this was coupled with a role as an officer, or as an executive committee member, or at least as a director. A lawyer with any sense paid close attention to his clients, cultivated them socially, and often became their close friend. Senior partners in the major firms were important members of the business community and were viewed as peers by the chief executive officers of the major businesses.

MARKETING

Law firms did not have formal marketing programs or staff in 1960, because they did not need them. Marketing was prohibited by the bar associations in all states. It was deemed a breach of the canons of ethics and grounds for discipline to solicit the business of another firm's client or to advertise. It just was not done.

Community service was one of the few ways that lawyers could cultivate relationships that might lead to new business. By working on a committee or as staff for a committee of prominent business leaders, lawyers could demonstrate their writing, speaking, and advocacy skills while earning the gratitude of business leaders. With luck, one would call on such lawyers for help with a paying project. Participating in a community project with an existing client could cement an important relationship for the firm.

One of my former colleagues told me of an experience he had in the late 1940s. He had worked on a civic project with the young chief executive officer of an important local business, someone with whom he had been acquainted since his school days. When the work was completed, the lawyer told the executive that he had enjoyed working with him on the project and would enjoy working with him more in the future. That afternoon, the young lawyer received a phone call from a senior partner in the firm that represented the executive's company. The senior partner said that the executive had told him of the comment made by the young lawyer, and he certainly hoped that the young lawyer had not intended by the comment to solicit any legal business from the client because, if so, the senior lawyer would be obligated to report the young lawyer to the disciplinary committee of the state bar for solicitation of another firm's client. The young lawyer assured the senior lawyer that he had no such intention, and his reference was only to further civic ventures. The chilling effect of such rules and their acceptance by clients and lawyers alike was significant. The rebuke still burned in the mind of my friend decades after the event.

As a result of such restrictions, the major firms tended to be very stable and their partners very secure. They could generally count on keeping the clients they had unless a client was acquired by another company or went bankrupt.

TYPES OF LEGAL SERVICES

Most firms in the corporate practice in Atlanta in the early sixties provided less than a full range of legal services to their clients. The Kilpatrick firm appears to have been the exception at that time. Several firms did not do labor work, and a few did not do tax work. Atlanta was blessed with several fine labor specialty firms, and one of the major firms had gotten its start doing tax work for firms that did not want to do tax work themselves. Many areas of practice that are important today, such as employment discrimination, foreign trade issues, immigration, environmental law, and health care, were insignificant or did not exist in Atlanta or elsewhere at that time.

SPECIALIZATION

Generally there were no departments of lawyers concentrating in particular areas of practice, and there were few lawyers specializing in only one area of practice.[7] Most were general business practitioners and provided a wide variety of services based on their clients' needs, although each tended to have one or more areas in which he had a higher level of expertise than some of his colleagues. Most lawyers would make some court appearances, and at some firms a few lawyers dealt only with litigation matters.

Because most of the partners were generalists and did not specialize, a young associate straight out of law school who had taken an up-to-date course in a particular area of the law would often be the most informed person in his firm on a subject. Specific expertise in a project was therefore often provided by younger lawyers, with senior lawyers playing a supervisory and client-relations role. Beginning associates were expected to do whatever work was needed by a client. I did everything from answering garnishments and representing the yard man of the CEO of the Citizens and Southern National Bank in the yard man's bankruptcy, to securities offerings and mergers and acquisitions.

ECONOMIC AND SOCIAL UNIFORMITY

All but one of the partners in the eight largest firms in Atlanta in 1960 were white men (the exception was a white woman), and

virtually all associates were men.[8] There were two female associates and no African American lawyers in these firms — the first
black lawyer was hired in 1969. Only three of the eight firms had
Jewish lawyers, and two of those with senior partners who were
Jewish had not employed a Jewish associate in a long time. The
other firms had a policy (sometimes public) of not hiring Jews,
and it never occurred to most of the firms to consider a woman or
a black. There was no apparent discrimination against Catholics,
although some firms did not have any. The Spaldings of Spalding,
Sibley, Troutman, Meadow & Smith were a prominent Catholic
family. It was standard procedure to ask law students interviewing
for a job to supply a letter of recommendation from their minis-
ters or Sunday school teachers.

One female associate in 1960 had been the secretary to a senior
partner in her firm and had obtained a law degree at night school.
During World War II when many of the firm's lawyers were serving in the armed forces, she filled in for them and continued to
practice when they returned. Her story was special enough to be
widely known.[9] The national picture for women was not much different: there were some 6,500 female lawyers in the United States
in 1960, or about 2.6 percent of the total. This percentage had remained essentially unchanged since 1951.[10]

It was usually the case in the early 1960s that most of the partners in these top eight Atlanta firms had come from middle- or
upper-class homes. At the Alston firm all five of the name partners came from prominent Georgia families, most of substantial
means, and they were all members of the Piedmont Driving Club,
the city's most exclusive social club.

Most of the young people entering the practice in the early
1960s liked the lifestyle and the community standing of the senior
partners and aspired to live at the same level of status and comfort. What many of those who were just starting out did not realize was that the majority of the senior partners they hoped to em-
ulate came from prosperous families and had financial resources
independent of their earnings from the practice of law.

THE FIRM FAMILY

Much emphasis was placed on the idea that a law firm was more than a business arrangement, and there was reverent use of the term *firm family*. Barring extreme circumstances such as death or disgrace, an affiliation with a law firm was like a marriage. It lasted a lifetime if you became a partner. Once part of a firm family, you found that it dominated not only your professional life but also your social life and that of your spouse. Many young associate couples who probably wished they were elsewhere made a foursome for bridge with senior partners and their wives on Saturday nights.

Aspects of an associate's personal life that are considered off-limits today were thought to be the firm's business in the sixties. At the Alston firm a summer associate showed up in 1969 sporting a small goatee that he had grown since his interview earlier in the year. One of the younger partners demanded of me as chairman of the recruiting committee that the summer associate shave it off or leave the firm by five o'clock that day. The partner insisted that clients would have no confidence in a man with hair on his face. I turned the demand aside, noting that one of our retired partners who still came to the office every day had worn a mustache since his graduation from the Harvard Law School in the 1920s. What was an accepted part of the appearance of a seventy-year-old lawyer was unacceptable for a younger man.

Until about 1970 no lawyer at the Alston firm had been divorced, and it was assumed that divorce would be grounds for termination. One day, while checking the references of a prospective associate, a senior partner and I discovered that the prospect was divorced. The senior partner immediately said that of course the prospect could not be considered further because he was divorced. Another senior partner overheard the discussion and said that since one of the firm's existing lawyers would be divorced in the near future (a secret that was being concealed at the time because of its sensational nature), to treat divorce as a bar to employment was going to have to be a thing of the past. Once a precedent had been established, several younger lawyers in the firm rushed to the divorce court.

Not only was the firm considered a family, but family ties were often very important in the firms. At Spalding, Sibley, Troutman, Meadow & Smith, senior partners Jimmy Sibley and Hughes Spalding had been preceded at the firm by their fathers, and in Mr. Spalding's case by his grandfather as well. At the Alston firm Philip H. Alston Jr. and James Alston were senior partners who had succeeded their uncle, Robert Cotton Alston, who had founded the firm, and their father, Philip Alston Sr. Known to all firm personnel as "Mr. Philip," Alston Sr. came to the office every day while in his early eighties. At Powell Goldstein, Elliott Goldstein had succeeded his father, Max, who still made regular appearances at the office in his eighties. Granger Hansell's son Ned and Robert Crenshaw's son Bob Jr. were following in their fathers' footsteps at Crenshaw, Hansell, Ware, Brandon & Dorsey. Hoke Smith had followed his father into Hirsch & Smith, known in 1960 as Smith, Kilpatrick, Cody, Rogers & McClatchey.

LATERAL HIRING

Lateral movement between Atlanta law firms did not occur in 1960. It was thought to be entirely inappropriate to hire a lawyer away from another major firm. Because the principals in these firms knew each other well and interacted both socially and in community affairs, it would have been ungentlemanly conduct to seek to take lawyers away from friends in another firm. It was simply not done. Furthermore, an associate terminated by a major firm would not have been hired by any of the others. Anyone not good enough for one would surely not have been good enough for another.

FIRM MANAGEMENT AND SUPPORT STAFF

There were generally three types of employees: partners, associates, and secretaries. Most of the firms were not large enough to require a full-time manager, and the secretary of one of the senior partners often served as a part-time office manager. Most firms would have had a bookkeeper. None had a librarian, and legal assistants did not yet exist, although many skilled secretaries performed this function. Firms were not interested in spending a lot of time and energy on management, in part because they were small but also because they did not feel the need to have managers formulating strategies to raise their profitability. In addition, minimal management afforded a good deal of autonomy to the partners, and they liked it that way.

TECHNOLOGY

Technology as we know it today in the practice of law did not exist. The only copying devices were Thermofax machines, which made a poor, smelly copy (often singed around the edges) from a loose page but could not copy a page from a book, because the page to be copied had to be fed into a narrow slot in the machine. All documents were produced on typewriters. Copies were made by use of carbon paper. A secretary who mistyped a single character had to erase each copy, usually messing up something else in the process. It took forever to type a contract with five carbon copies. If you needed ten copies, you had to type it twice. If you wanted to add a paragraph at the beginning, you had to retype the whole thing. As a result, document production was a slow and cumbersome process. Your only alternative for long documents was to use a professional printer, and most clients felt that was too expensive for frequent use. Consequently, lawyers did not lightly suggest that something in a typed agreement be changed unless it was really important. This discouraged constant negotiating. It also encouraged shorter briefs, contracts, and other documents.

Dictating machines were coming into widespread use, though many of the senior partners still dictated to the secretaries who took shorthand. Telephones had none of the special features we have come to expect today. There was no conferencing capability except by special arrangement with the telephone company, and primitive speaker phones did not arrive until the late 1960s. There were no voice mail machines to record messages or to give them, and there were no fax machines. My first experience with a fax machine was in the mid-1970s when an urgent document was faxed to me from London. Somehow it ended up on the Master-Card fax of the Citizens and Southern Bank of South Carolina from whence it found its way to my office a week later when it was of no use.

There was no Federal Express or similar private mail service so that, with rare exceptions, correspondence and documents were delivered to other parties by the U.S. Postal Service, which was generally believed to be more reliable than it is thought to be today. Travel by train or car took even longer in 1960 than it does today; the interstate highway system had not been completed. Jet airplanes were relatively new, and prop planes were much slower than today's aircraft. Air travel was considered expensive; there were fewer flights and longer flight times. Many people then were afraid of flying. Because travel was slow, it was time-consuming and difficult to hold meetings that involved people from different locations, and lawyers attended fewer meetings in cities away from home. Trains were still used for business travel in those days, and I have many pleasant memories of train trips to New York. "The Southerner" left Atlanta's Terminal Station about 1 P.M. each day, providing excellent meals in its dining car. You reached Pennsylvania Station the next morning around 9 A.M.

These various obstacles to document production, transportation, and communication placed a premium on brevity and on reaching agreement expeditiously. They discouraged meetings and changes in documents. As a result, they conspired to hold down, rather than to increase, legal costs.

WORK PRODUCT REUSE

One of the advantages of a law firm is its ability to accumulate and utilize the various experiences of its lawyers. Frequently it is possible to reuse a document in producing a new one, which saves time and money and produces better quality because the new document has the benefit of the tested use of the old one. In the early sixties, firms had not begun to worry about storing and reusing their historical work product. The firms were small enough so that most of the lawyers knew the work that the firm had done and in whose office the documents could be found. It was not uncommon to make the rounds of the partners until you found one who had the experience or knowledge that you needed and would discuss the problem with you. As the firms grew in the midsixties, they began to think about maintaining files of forms and memoranda, which would permit any lawyer in the firm to retrieve the work product of the other lawyers. Of course, there was no computerized legal research. Because there were few textbooks (there were more in tax than in any other area), lawyers relied heavily on reported cases for knowledge as well as for precedent.

FACILITIES

In Atlanta, the offices of major business practice law firms were adequate but far from imposing. At most firms, clients would enter a small reception room with seating for four or five people and would be greeted by a receptionist who also operated the telephone switchboard. When I first joined the Alston firm, the reception room had two windows opening onto an air shaft, and the furniture in the room could charitably be described as well used. As the Alston firm began to require much more office space, it used the interior design services of the firm's client, Sears Roebuck, to redecorate the reception area.

Both partners' and associates' offices were somewhat smaller than the average office today. Wood paneling and wallpaper were rare, and there were few built-in bookcases and cabinets. There was no need for ostentatious interior stairwells or two-story lobbies with Italian marble or other costly embellishments because each firm only occupied a floor or less in its building. The men's and women's restrooms were often on alternating floors and, in the case of the Alston firm, the men's room was on the floor below our offices outside the front door of one of our competitors, Powell Goldstein Frazer & Murphy. As a result the lawyers in both firms knew one another well.

The firms did not have kitchens or break rooms. Most did not have coffee service available in the office. We went out to lunch every day, and one of the firm's senior partners led a group to the cafeteria of the Citizens and Southern National Bank, our largest client and landlord, for a twenty-minute coffee break twice a day.

IN-HOUSE LEGAL STAFFS

Hardly any clients had in-house legal staff in 1960. Not a single company for which the Alston firm was principal legal counsel had an in-house lawyer. The firm provided most of the legal services that its principal clients required, perhaps with special counsel on occasion. Major local companies usually called upon a senior partner in a major firm to serve as their senior legal adviser and counsel. Indeed, this was the type of position to which all the younger lawyers aspired. Senior partners in the Alston firm held such positions with Genuine Parts Company, Magic Chef, Inc., and the Citizens and Southern National Bank. Often senior partners also served on the client's board of directors and its executive committee. In 1960, a few major Atlanta companies such as Coca-Cola and Southern Bell had small legal departments and an in-house general counsel, but they were exceptions to the rule.[11]

GROWTH IN THE 1960S

Serious economic growth arrived in Atlanta in the mid-1960s shortly after the arrival of an activist Democratic administration in January 1961. As a result, by the midsixties the major business practice firms were growing in response to a growing economy and increased government regulation, which caused businesses to seek more legal assistance. The firms spontaneously took advantage of the opportunity without much forethought as to the impact such growth would have on them and on the legal profession. None foresaw the extent or consequences of the growth that would occur.

2 Economic Growth – Dynamic Change

I n the mid-1960s, as economic activity increased, all major Atlanta law firms serving business clients expanded to serve the increasing needs of existing clients and a growing roster of new ones. The hiring of partners or associates from other firms was rare and was disparaged by all firms, so the only way a firm could provide the additional services needed by its growing clientele was to work its lawyers harder and to hire at the entry level more new associates to be brought along as quickly as possible.

Because revenues produced by the additional associates substantially exceeded their costs, firms soon found their net incomes increasing and were able to pay all partners higher compensation.

This increase in the number of associates relative to the number of partners is generally referred to as an increase in the associate-partner ratio, or increased associate leverage.

Having discovered the profitability of higher associate-partner ratios and with sufficient new business to support them, the firms continued to grow and prosper, annually hiring additional associates. New associates were hired not only to replace those who had become partners or had departed the firm but also to increase the total number and percentage of associates working for each firm. This process increased associate leverage.

GROWTH AND ASSOCIATE LEVERAGE

At the end of the sixties, the largest firm in Atlanta was still the Hansell firm, by then known as Hansell, Post, Brandon & Dorsey, the name that resulted from the merger in 1962 of Crenshaw, Hansell, Ware, Brandon & Dorsey and Moise, Post & Gardner. It had grown from twenty-one lawyers in 1960 to fifty-three in 1970, of whom thirty-five were partners and eighteen were associates. Some of the growth had come from the addition of six Moise, Post & Gardner partners. Only two associates had moved to the Hansell firm from the Moise firm.

During the 1960s, Spalding, Sibley, Troutman, Meadow & Smith changed its name to King & Spalding and grew from ten partners and five associates to twenty-two partners and eighteen associates in 1970. Powell Goldstein had thirty-seven lawyers in 1970, of whom seventeen were associates. Smith, Kilpatrick, Cody, Rogers & McClatchey changed its name to Kilpatrick, Cody, Rogers, McClatchey & Regenstein and grew from seven partners and nine associates to eighteen partners and eighteen associates. The Alston firm changed its name in 1962 to Alston, Miller & Gaines as a result of the acquisition of three new partners and two associates from another firm – the first important lateral move among the major Atlanta firms in that decade.

By 1970, the Alston firm had grown from ten partners and five associates to nineteen partners and fifteen associates. The Alston firm expanded its operations by opening a small Washington, D.C., office in 1967 with the addition of two partners and two associates. In doing this they joined the company of another major Atlanta firm, Sutherland, Asbill & Brennan, which had originated in Atlanta, opened and then closed a Washington office before World War II, and reopened after the war. Sutherland had forty-one lawyers in 1970, of whom twenty-three were in Atlanta.

Troutman Sanders did not yet exist in its present form. Its predecessor firm, Troutman, Sams, Schroder & Lockerman, had twelve partners and three associates. It had become ripe for acquisition by the growing firm of former governor Carl Sanders, and a merger of these firms took place in 1971. The associate leverage of the seven largest Atlanta firms had increased slightly during the 1960s from 0.6:1 in 1960 to 0.7:1 in 1970, reflecting the fact that the average firm still had considerably more partners than associates.

By 1980, King & Spalding had become the largest law firm in Atlanta, with 102 lawyers of whom 52 were partners and 50 associates. During the 1970s, the Hansell firm had grown from 40 to 97 lawyers (from 22 partners and 18 associates to 54 partners, 42 associates, and one counsel).[1] The Alston firm had grown from 34 lawyers to 74 in Atlanta (from 19 partners and 15 associates to 35 partners and 39 associates) and the firm's Washington office contributed another 10 for a total of 84. The firm's growth was adversely affected by the withdrawal at various times of several partners including the four who left in 1977 to form Trotter, Bondurant, Griffin, Miller & Hishon. The Kilpatrick firm had grown from 36 lawyers to 77 (from 18 partners and 18 associates to 35 partners and 42 associates). Powell, Goldstein, Frazer & Murphy grew to 92 lawyers of whom 39 were partners and 53 associates. Troutman Sanders had 25 partners and 40 associates, and Sutherland had 60 partners and 56 associates in its two offices.

The average ratio of associates to partners of the seven largest Atlanta firms had increased significantly from about 0.7:1 in 1970 to slightly more than 1:1 in 1980,[2] reflecting the increasing associate leverage that contributed to the profitability of these firms. Approximately 8 to 9 percent of these lawyers were women. The percentage of female and African American partners in 1980 was negligible: in Atlanta firms with over fifty attorneys in 1977, only one out of every 100 partners was a woman,[3] and there was only one black partner in 1980.

The 1980s witnessed a further growth in the size of the major firms in Atlanta and throughout the nation and further growth in their associate leverage as well. The largest firm in Atlanta in 1990 was King & Spalding with 243 lawyers, of whom 105 were partners and 138 associates or counsel, and an associate-partner ratio of 1.31:1. Alston & Bird (the result of the merger in 1982 of Alston, Miller & Gaines and Jones, Bird & Howell) had 194 lawyers of whom 82 were partners and 112 associates (1.37:1). Powell Goldstein had grown to 74 partners and 84 associates by 1990 (1.14:1), whereas Kilpatrick & Cody languished with 53 partners and 70 associates (1.32:1). The average associate leverage ratio for the firms in the sample for 1990 is 1.3:1.[4] Figure 2.1 illustrates the increasing associate leverage over the three decades.

The demand for legal services continued to expand in the Southeast during the early 1990s, and the major firms based in Atlanta continued to grow and to extend their national and international presence. By 1995 King & Spalding had become the fifty-fourth largest law firm in America with 345 lawyers (a 42 percent increase from 1990); Alston & Bird had 308 lawyers (a 60 percent increase); Sutherland, Asbill & Brennan had 275; Powell, Goldstein, Frazer & Murphy had 226; Kilpatrick & Cody had 210 (a 70 percent increase); and Troutman Sanders had 189. All six of the major Atlanta-based firms that survived from 1960 were among the 163 largest firms in the United States in 1995.

The eighties were also a period of growth in the number of female attorneys in Atlanta. By 1987 women accounted for 5 percent of the partners in firms with 50 or more lawyers. In firms with over 10 lawyers, 64 of the 1,227 partners in the city in 1987 were women.[5]

FIGURE 2.1 AVERAGE ASSOCIATE-
PARTNER RATIO IN ATLANTA, 1960—1995

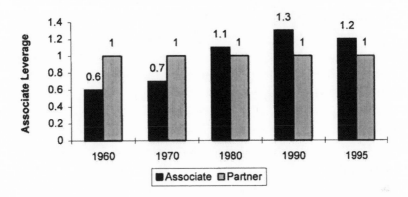

THE EMERGENCE OF THE HOURLY RATE SYSTEM

During the late sixties and early seventies, most major firms started charging for their services based on the amount of time spent by the firm's lawyers on a project. Each lawyer was assigned an hourly rate that was charged to the clients, and the rate was usually based on seniority in practice. Most firms also adopted the practice of regularly increasing rates of individual lawyers based on their years of experience. Under these schedules the rates of individual associates would increase five or ten dollars every six months or every year during their first several years of practice, and as they became more senior, rates would increase by a similar amount every two or three years.

Partner rates were higher and increased every three to five years (by $25 to $50) before a senior partner reached his maximum rate level at around the age of fifty. Firms experimented with multiple rate structures that provided for a lawyer having a higher hourly rate in his area of special expertise. If a lawyer moved up from one category to a more senior one at the same time that his firm's rates were being increased across the board, his rate could increase substantially in a single year.

Rate schedules turned out to be a boon for law firms when price controls were imposed by the federal government in the early seventies, because seniority-based increases that were a part of preexisting schedules and practices were allowed, although across-the-board increases were prohibited. After price controls were ended in the mid-1970s, a firm's rates were often increased annually across the board in response to inflation and the market's willingness to bear higher rates. The high inflation of the late seventies conditioned American businesses to substantial annual increases in costs and set the stage for significant rate increases in the legal profession during the 1980s, even though the inflation that gave rise to such expectations had diminished.

In Atlanta, hourly rates were first insisted upon by in-house general counsel of major national corporations beginning in the 1960s, although the shift from retainers and other non–time-based billing was not completed until the 1970s. Previously firms had determined their fees using imprecise formulas, often charging more when the results of their efforts were especially good. As national clients began to push their outside firms to hourly rates, firms inquired about the possibility of charging a premium for good results, but were normally told that the client felt it had hired the best firm available and expected a good result for the rate it had agreed to pay, and consequently did not believe that good results should cost extra. Most firms were not happy when their clients required them to base their charges solely on hourly rates. They acquiesced to the change because their clients required it. They did not realize at the time the bonanza that awaited them under such an hourly rate system.

YOU ARE WHAT YOU BILL

By 1980, the major firms in Atlanta were all keeping track of the billable time of each lawyer. Billable time became a critical part of each firm's budgeting process and the most useful analytical tool in evaluating firm economic performance and prospects. Somewhere along the way many lawyers began to confuse their role in selling legal products and services with selling time, and they began to divorce considerations of quality, efficiency, and results from the hours invested in the effort.

A senior partner of a prominent firm wrote to me after my speech to the corporate counsel section of the state bar:

> You may not have put quite enough emphasis on maintaining billable hours. We started logging hours as a means of refreshing our memories for help in determining the value of our services. We did not have hourly rates by which to multiply time spent. On most routine matters which frequently encompassed the drawing of a will, the creation of a corporation for a sole proprietor, etc., there were fixed rates which we quoted in advance and charged when we were through.
>
> As time passed, keeping of records of time changed their tenor as a billing aid to a measure of the work done by a lawyer. If you can do in one hour what I do in five, unless there is a pretty critical judge comparing our work, I am thought to be five times more valuable than you. It is here that I believe we began to lose sight of ourselves as members of a profession in search of justice and fair dealing among our clients, the public generally and ourselves in favor of a business organized for the sale of a service at the highest price.[6]

When the Alston firm began keeping track of time, there was no thought of keeping track of the aggregate billable hours of individual lawyers nor were there expectations that each lawyer would meet a quota of billable time each year. The hours were not tabulated for that purpose. The work for each day was recorded on a separate time slip for each client for whom work had been performed, and the slips were maintained by client matter in chronological order by a clerk. When a matter was ripe for billing, the clerk would add up the time for each lawyer. The billing attorney would peruse the slips, prepare a general description of the work performed, and determine the amount of the fee based, in part, on the time invested by each lawyer who had worked on the project and his billable rate. But he would also take into account such factors as the complexity of the matter, the result obtained, and the value in the transaction. As time went on, more and more clients expected to be billed based on time alone, and the law firms became accustomed to thinking about the bill in the same way.

In due course it occurred to someone that the time billed by each lawyer had an impact on the firm's profitability and that each lawyer's value to the firm was at least in part related to the number of hours he billed and to the rate at which his time was charged. Consequently, most firms began keeping track of the total billable hours of individual lawyers shortly after they started keeping track of the lawyer time invested in individual client matters. It was then that the firms came face to face with the fact that some lawyers were putting in a lot more billable time than others, which was easier to ignore when no one was keeping an official tally.

In the midsixties some of the associates at the Alston firm became aware that the billing clerk was no longer just organizing the time slips chronologically by client matter and adding up the time invested in each matter by individual lawyers so that this information could be used in the billing process. The clerk was also adding up the total time recorded by each lawyer for all the work done during the year and reporting it to firm management. Not surprisingly this occurred shortly after the firm hired its first outside law firm management consultant and appointed its first managing partner. This realization set the stage for an emotional protest about the keeping of these records and their use. This protest became known in firm folklore as the "bacon and eggs rebellion," because it occurred one fine spring Saturday morning when the senior partner, Philip Alston, had invited all of the associates for a breakfast visit at the beautiful new home he had just built in Atlanta's Ansley Park.

Several associates called a meeting the night before to discuss issues of concern to them and to plan the next morning's unscheduled presentation of their concerns to Mr. Alston, who was the firm's dominant partner. Although I had been unaware of these time records, I was the senior associate present at the meeting (the "SAP," as I was soon to discover), and I was asked to be the spokesman and make the presentation to Mr. Alston on behalf of the associates, most of whom felt strongly about the matter. They believed that keeping track of such information and using it to evaluate both associates and partners for the purposes of advancement and compensation would lead to competition among the lawyers to put in the most hours and that such considerations as quality of work and time spent on community service would be sacrificed.

Serving as the spokesman for the associates had its disadvantages. Although I did not personally agree with all of the ideas put forward, I was blamed for all of them. Several of my fellow associates who had been most vocal the night before were conspicuous by their silence during the meeting with Mr. Alston and thereafter. Many of the ideas were unpopular with various partners. One of the younger partners, who was among those criticized by the associates for his perceived role in the timekeeping decision, was a good friend of mine. On the Monday morning after the "rebellion" he called me into his office and with considerable emotion told me that he understood I was an "articulate spokesman for the basic proposition" that he was "a first-class son of a bitch." We have weathered that storm and remain friends.

After the breakfast protest by the associates, the partners deliberated about what the appropriate policy ought to be, and the practice of reviewing the billable time of individual lawyers was dropped by the Alston firm for more than ten years. Because the firm had plenty of work and was growing, and because the partners were enjoying an increased level of income they had not anticipated, they agreed that such timekeeping practices would undermine the firm's close-knit culture, and they saw no need to encourage competition among the lawyers.

ANNUAL BILLABLE TIME EXPECTATIONS

It is difficult to evaluate precisely the increase in the amount of billable time and the working hours of lawyers in Atlanta between 1960 and 1990 because the major firms did not keep statistics for individual lawyers in the early 1960s. However, having retained my own time records from my first days of practice, I know that I had approximately 1,300 recorded billable hours in 1964 and 1,100 in 1965. My billable hours tended to be on the low side because of a heavier than average load of administrative responsibilities and civic involvements, but I believe that 1,400 to 1,500 recorded billable hours was an acceptable load for many associates in Atlanta in those days.

Some variation occurs from firm to firm, with the more demanding firms expecting longer hours, including many nights and weekends, devoted to the practice. A senior partner who was an associate at Kilpatrick & Cody in 1960 believes that associates in his day put in more hours at the office than associates do today, and I know that they worked harder than we did at the Alston firm. In any event, it would have been very unusual for an associate to record 2,000 billable hours a year in the midsixties. It is important to note that timekeeping practices were different from what they are today, and many working hours devoted to client affairs went unrecorded. In any event, not all time recorded on matters for clients was deemed to be "billable."

By the early 1990s most major business practice firms in Atlanta expected their lawyers to record 1,800 to 1,900 billable hours, and some expected more from their associates. Most partners at most major firms are now expected to record 1,600 to 1,900 billable hours a year. There are, of course, always exceptions to the rule. At the same time, in New York City, many of the major business practice firms have admitted publicly to expecting up to 2,100 billable hours a year from associates,[7] and it is a poorly kept secret that many really expect a good many more.

BILLING RATES

Very little information exists about billing rates in Atlanta in the early 1960s, because many firms did not keep track of time and therefore had no need for hourly rates. Those that did were not inclined to talk about it. The Alston firm was unusual in this respect, because one of the senior partners of the firm had worked for Davis, Polk & Wardwell in New York before World War II. When he came to the Alston firm after the war, he brought "advanced management techniques" including the recording of time and hourly rates, all of which were in place when I arrived in the summer of 1960. For those clients that insisted on being billed at hourly rates, the Alston firm billed a new associate at $20, a new partner at $35, and a senior partner at $60 an hour.

Billing rates increased during the sixties so that by 1970 a starting associate was billed at $25 an hour (a 25 percent increase from $20 an hour in 1962); a junior partner at $50 an hour; a senior partner at $90 an hour (representing a 50 percent increase if you assume a $60 hourly rate in 1962). The highest partner rate was 2.4 times the starting associate rate.

By 1980, new associates in these Atlanta firms were billed at $45 to $60 an hour (an 80–140 percent increase over 1970); junior partners were billed at $80 to $100 an hour (a 60–100 percent increase); senior partners at $140 to $150 an hour (a 56–67 percent increase); all of this occurred in a decade when inflation had been about 98 percent.[8] Senior partner rates increased less than the rates of associates and junior partners, and they also increased less than inflation, with the result that senior partners became a relatively better value than the other lawyers in a firm.

The high inflation of the late 1970s proved to be an unexpected boon in the years ahead. During the late seventies, American businesses learned to expect inflation and to live with it, and this attitude carried forward into the eighties, although the rate of inflation declined. During the 1980s, law firms found they could increase their hourly rates to exceed inflation without receiving objections from their clients.

By 1990, new associates were billed at $80 to $90 per hour in Atlanta (an increase of 50 – 78 percent during the eighties); new partners at $165 to $175 per hour (an increase of 75 – 89 percent over 1980 hourly rates of $80 to $100); and senior partners at $265 to $275 per hour (an increase of 83 – 89 percent); all of this occurred in a decade in which inflation had been approximately 71 percent.[9] By 1995, rates for beginning associates were $110 an hour, for first-year partners $200 an hour, and $315 to $325 for the most expensive partners. These increases essentially kept pace with inflation during the first half of the 1990s. Figure 2.2 shows the hourly rates for Atlanta firms in 1962 compared with the rates in effect in 1970 and as they would have been had they been adjusted only for inflation. A similar comparison is made for the 1970s, 1980s, and early 1990s.

Over the three and a half decades billing rates increased somewhat in excess of inflation. Because partner billing rates increased in excess of inflation in the eighties, lawyers at all levels were recording more billable time, and associate leverage was increasing, partner compensation skyrocketed. (See chapter 4.)

The Price of Legal Services

The fees charged by the Alston firm for various sorts of legal projects in 1970 – 1971 included $35,000 to organize a real estate investment trust and to represent it in an initial public offering of its securities (a fee that was heavily negotiated and did not represent the full cost of the project on an hourly rate basis); $61,500 for a similar project for another client that was paid at the full hourly rate (described as a "home run" by a very pleased senior partner); $1,050 to prepare an annual meeting proxy statement for a company whose securities were traded over the counter; $15,400 for an S-1 registration statement for a client in an initial

FIGURE 2.2 HOURLY RATES FOR BEGINNING ASSOCIATES,
BEGINNING PARTNERS, AND SENIOR PARTNERS IN ATLANTA, 1962–1995,
AND RATES AS ADJUSTED FOR INFLATION

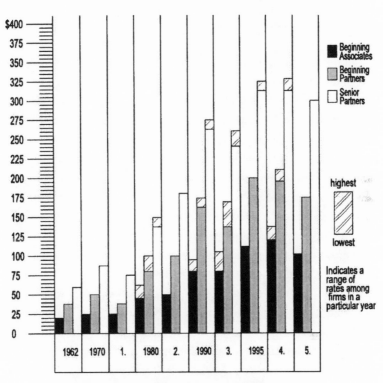

1. 1962 adjusted for inflation of 24% in the 1960s.
2. 1970 adjusted for inflation of 98% in the 1970s.
3. 1980 adjusted for inflation of 71% in the 1980s.
4. 1990 adjusted for inflation of 20% between 1990 and 1994.
5. 1962 adjusted for inflation of 401.5% 1960–1994.

public offering; $3,500 to represent the underwriters in a private placement of utility bonds to institutional investors; $9,000 to represent an underwriter in a registered public offering of securities; $20,000 to represent an issuer in an underwritten public offering of subordinated debt; and $12,000 to represent an issuer in an underwritten public offering of common stock.[10] Inflation has been approximately 282 percent since 1970. These charges can be compared with charges today by applying a factor of four, which would slightly overstate the impact of inflation between 1970 and 1995.

COMPENSATION

Compensation increased significantly in excess of inflation for associates and partners alike throughout most of the sixties, seventies, and eighties. Initially, the increases occurred as a natural result of the growth in the demand for legal services, which was met by the addition of younger and less experienced lawyers. This resulted in a significant increase in associate leverage and in income for the partners in the major firms. Once big-firm lawyers had become accustomed to higher compensation, they became addicted to it and craved more. In due course, big incomes attracted young people interested in big incomes. By the late 1980s, compensation had become the dominant force shaping most major law firms and how they practiced law.

Because of the structure of the legal profession, it was inevitable that greatly increased profitability would come about when the firms started growing rapidly to meet the increased demand for legal services. It was a natural result of having a growing cadre of young lawyers working at relatively low salaries who were generating billable hours chargeable to clients at substantial profit margins. In the process, firms that had been operating for years with a ratio of several partners to each associate found themselves with one, or two, or in some cases three or four associates working and generating profits for each partner.

After the increased leverage ratios had been established, any reduction in the ratio should have had the effect of reducing profits for the partners, unless the lawyers in the firm put in even more billable hours or the hourly rates were raised in excess of inflation. Once the partners became accustomed to this newfound profitability, it became the accepted norm, and the firms became dependent on associate leverage to maintain profitability. Then during the early 1990s, associate leverage at most of the major

Atlanta firms declined, but average profits per partner did not drop. Some firms achieved this modern miracle in part by creating a category of nonequity partners who in effect work for a salary. The firms also achieved more billable hours and higher rates to sustain and increase partner profitability.

INFLATION

Throughout this book I have endeavored to compare billable rates and compensation from the beginning of the 1960s through 1994 in inflation-adjusted dollars.[11] This is the only way in which it is possible to truly understand what has occurred in the legal profession since 1960.

Inflation (as calculated by the U.S. government and reflected in the Consumer Price Index (CPI) was 24 percent in the 1960s, 98 percent in the 1970s, 71 percent in the 1980s, and 20 percent from 1990 through 1994.[12] The cumulative inflation from 1960 to 1994 has been approximately 401 percent. The CPI is not a perfect tool to use as a basis of comparison, but it is the best we have. The various costs used in computing the index and their relative weight in the process have changed over time. Some very important costs to lawyers in Atlanta have increased at a rate greater than the CPI during the last thirty-five years, most significantly the cost of homes, automobiles, and educating children.

There is a tendency to dismiss historical comparisons on the grounds that changes in the value of the dollar have rendered comparisons useless. In fact, it provides an excuse for avoiding a thoughtful analysis of the implications of current compensation levels.

TECHNOLOGY

During the mid-1960s, the Xerox photocopier made possible the "cut and paste" approach to document production, which significantly increased the speed with which a document could be revised. In due course, "mag card" typewriters and then computerized word processing carried the day. However, as late as the mid-1970s the typewriter was still viewed at most firms as the principal document production tool. Firms that had computerized word processing often confined it to the word processing center or required secretaries to share computer terminals.

During the late 1970s, the arrival of the first generation of law graduates trained on computers further confused the picture. Naturally these young lawyers wanted to compose their own work directly at the computer screen, but to do so they had to displace their secretaries because only secretaries had terminals at their desks. Many a senior partner was annoyed by associates "doing secretarial work" and preventing the secretaries from doing their own jobs. Now most younger lawyers and many older ones in large firms have their own computer terminals and are connected to their secretaries and colleagues through the firms' networks.

DIVERSITY

Major Atlanta firms began to hire female associates in the late 1960s. The Alston firm's first woman associate was hired in 1968 to do residential loan closing work, an area of practice thought to be beneath the talent of most male lawyers at most major firms. The second female associate, Orinda Evans, was hired in 1969, and she insisted on work in the mainstream of the firm's practice. In due course, she became a successful litigator, a partner, and a federal district court judge. She remains the only lawyer to have been appointed to the federal bench from the Alston firm.

In 1969 the Alston firm hired its first black associate, John L. Kennedy, a graduate of Morehouse College and the Harvard Law School and son of a Morehouse College professor. Kennedy left the firm after about two years and in due course founded one of Atlanta's leading African American firms: Thomas, Kennedy, Sampson, Edwards & Patterson. The same year that the Alston firm hired Kennedy, another old Atlanta firm hired Prentiss Q. Yancey Jr., a black graduate of the Emory University Law School who was a member of a locally prominent family. Yancey became a partner with Smith, Cohen, Ringel, Kohler, Martin & Lowe in 1975 and has remained with his original firm, now known as Smith, Gambrell & Russell. The Alston firm also hired its first black summer associate in 1969, Melvin Watt, from the Yale Law School. He decided to practice in Charlotte, North Carolina, and after a successful career as a lawyer was elected to Congress in 1992.

By the early 1970s, discrimination against Jews by the major firms was a thing of the past. In the 1960s the Kilpatrick firm was the only major Atlanta firm with several Jewish lawyers. Two other firms with senior partners who were Jewish had not hired Jewish associates in many years. However, they hired lateral-entry associates who were Jewish in the 1960s, and several of the major firms hired new associates who were Jewish in the late 1960s. The Alston firm's first Jewish associate joined the firm in 1970.

NEW LAWYER SUPPLY AND DEMAND

During the sixties, the major Atlanta firms were able to hire law review students from the top local and regional law schools and students from the top quarter to the top third of their classes at the national schools, including Harvard and Yale. Many of these students were southerners who were attracted to Atlanta by its more progressive racial policies and its more vigorous economic growth. These same students were highly sought after by other major business practice firms in the United States.

As the law firms began to grow and to hire more young lawyers, there were not enough top students to meet the firms' needs, even with law school enrollment climbing 41 percent between 1967 and 1971. First-year law school enrollment increased from 20,776 in

FIGURE 2.3 FIRST-YEAR CLASS
LAW SCHOOL ENROLLMENT, 1963–1994

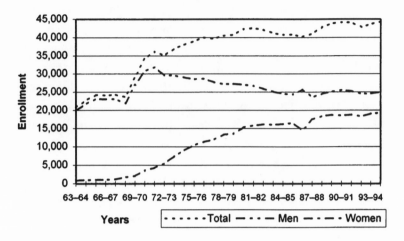

the 1963 – 64 academic year to 24,267 in 1967 – 68; to 36,171 in 1971 – 72; to 40,717 in 1979 – 80. First-year enrollment reached 42,521 in 1981 – 82 and did not exceed that number until 1988 – 89, when enrollment reached 42,860 (Figure 2.3). First-year enrollment has since increased to 44,298 in 1994 – 95.

From 1963 – 64 to 1994 – 95, the number of accredited law schools increased from 135 to 177, enrollment increased by 113 percent, and the enrollment of women in the first-year class soared from 877 to 19,312, up 2,200 percent. The number of male first-year law students peaked in 1971 – 72 at 31,845 and fell to 24,986 in 1994 – 95, down 22 percent.[13] In 1994 – 95, women accounted for 44 percent of the total first year enrollment of 44,298 students.

Over time, despite such growth, there simply was not enough top talent to go around, and everyone compromised to some extent. Demand for new graduates continued to rise more rapidly than law school enrollment during the 1970s, forcing the major law firms to reduce their quality standards and reach lower into the law school classes.

I remember well the 1972 recruiting season at the Alston firm. I served as chairman of the recruiting committee. We were suffering a real shortage of lawyer capacity in the firm, and there was serious talk for the first time of turning down the business of attractive clients because of the lack of qualified lawyers. This situation put a strain on the partnership. If some potentially valuable clients were to be turned away, whose would those be, how would it be decided, and by whom? If the personnel shortage were to continue, how would the firm's associates be allocated, and to whose clients?

After the first round of cuts of prospective associates, we were substantially short of the new lawyers we felt we needed. The recruiting committee was taken to task for being too elitist and was directed to reconsider the top portion of the group of students who we felt were not up to our historic standards and to whom we had not offered jobs. As a result of that review, we decided to extend offers to several students who had been cut initially, and most of those offers were accepted. None of those added to the list eventually became partners. In the meantime, the trend toward lower standards had begun.

The firms also responded by raising their compensation to attract the best of the available graduates. Unfortunately for the firms, particularly during the 1980s, significantly increased compensation did not have a corresponding impact on the number and quality of students attending law school. The Alston firm, along with its competitors, responded by developing new and more aggressive recruiting programs, which included lavish and artificial summer programs and more aggressive promotional literature, and by increasing the number of schools to which the firm sent recruiters.

The firms have generally followed the policy of paying all newly graduated lawyers the same starting salary. The substantial increases in starting salaries (and related increases up the line, which were not necessarily done at the same percentage rate) had their origins as premium pay for the best and brightest law students, but in due course became premium pay for everybody.

The Atlanta firms did not formally agree among themselves to new salary levels. They usually waited until one of their competitors announced an increase, and then the others quickly followed. This practice continued until Jones, Day, Reavis & Pogue arrived on the scene from out of town and acquired Hansell & Post in 1989. Jones, Day started paying a higher starting salary than the other Atlanta firms, but the others did not feel the necessity of matching that higher salary and did not respond to Jones, Day initiatives.

Exceptions are usually made for judicial clerks, who are given longevity credit for their time as clerks. As a result of this practice, U.S. Supreme Court clerks, who are the most pursued of the law school graduates, receive the highest starting pay because they have usually clerked for three years or more. As a practical matter, the Supreme Court justices require that all applicants for their clerkships have clerked for one or two years with a federal Court of Appeals judge before applying for a Supreme Court position. This extended clerkship time also provides the firms an excuse for paying these lawyers a greater salary than other beginning associates.

Most Supreme Court clerks take jobs in Washington or New York. A high percentage of them become law professors. I am aware of only five Supreme Court clerks who have practiced law in Atlanta in the last thirty-five years. Four of them practiced at the same time with Trotter, Bondurant, Miller & Hishon in the early 1980s. Of the five, two have become law school professors elsewhere, two are in private practice in Atlanta, and one is the in-house general counsel of a technology company in Norcross, Georgia.

LATERAL MOVES

There was little lateral movement involving the seven major Atlanta business practice firms in the 1960s. The move of Alex Gaines, two of his younger partners, and two associates to the Alston firm in 1962 from another significant Atlanta firm (but not one of the seven largest) was the first lateral move of important partners from one Atlanta firm to another in the postwar period, but it was viewed by many as something of a merger and therefore not a breach of the legal community ethic against lateral moves. The 1960s saw few situations where a partner left a major firm to start a new firm, and when it did happen, the new firms did not have a significant impact on the legal landscape.

The 1970s saw an increase in lateral activity with the movement of a few significant younger partners from one major firm to another as the taboo against this behavior gradually broke down. The seventies also witnessed the departure of an increasing number of partners from major Atlanta firms to establish new firms or branch offices for national firms, and these firms grew in part by attracting disgruntled partners and associates from other major firms.

These lateral moves were made possible by the growth in the major firms, which pushed responsibility for new clients down to younger partners, who then had the capacity to move their clients with them and to increase their compensation in the process. Long, Aldridge & Norman, a firm of 113 lawyers in 1995 (fifty-two partners, sixty-one associates and counsel) and the seventh largest firm in Atlanta, is the most successful of these new firms, some of which did not survive. The Atlanta office of Paul, Hastings, Janofsky & Walker of Los Angeles, with nineteen partners, thirty-six associates, and four counsel in 1995, and the office of Hunton & Williams of Richmond with sixteen partners, twenty associates, and one counsel are the largest of the branch offices of national firms in Atlanta after Jones, Day.[14]

Despite change, growth, and the appearance of some important new firms, the major Atlanta business practice firms from 1960 maintained their strength and position with the exception of Hansell & Post, Atlanta's largest firm for almost thirty years. The firm was racked by dissention and defections in the mideighties and became the Atlanta office of Jones, Day, Reavis & Pogue in 1989, at a much reduced size of 104 lawyers. It shrank further to seventy-eight lawyers in 1993 but rebounded to ninety lawyers in 1995.[15]

THE IN-HOUSE REVOLUTION

As the need for legal advice became an everyday matter in the 1970s, and as costs began to rise, clients began to hire lawyers as employees to meet the legal service needs of their businesses. Initially, most companies hired one lawyer who spent most of his or her time assigning work to, and sometimes supervising the work of, outside lawyers. There were advantages to the client in having a lawyer who worked exclusively on the company's affairs and who was housed with other company executives. The lawyer was more likely to be available, or to be found on short notice, without conflicting demands on his or her time and attention. House counsel was also more likely to have an understanding of the client's business because of greater exposure to personnel and business operations.

Later in the seventies, the size of in-house staffs began to increase and in-house lawyers began doing some of the work previously performed by outside counsel. Initially, this work tended to be the most routine legal work such as preparation of corporate minutes, qualifications to do business, and recurring operational issues such as, in the case of a bank, small loans and questions concerning checks. As the in-house departments grew, they expanded their areas of responsibility and thereby reduced the work for which outside counsel was required.

Growth of in-house staff became a major factor in Atlanta in the late 1970s and 1980s. The growing need for legal advice and the increasing cost of using outside counsel caused most major companies and many smaller ones to hire lawyers to work full-time as their employees. This in-house revolution is one of the most significant changes in the practice of law to occur in the United States since 1960. By 1990 many in-house staffs handled the bulk of the legal needs of their companies. Outside counsel was needed only for specialized matters that did not justify the maintenance in-house of the necessary expertise or for major matters that required more lawyer time than was available when added to the ongoing responsibilities of the in-house staff. Litigation often fell into the latter category. Issues concerning admission to practice in the various states also resulted in use of outside counsel in connection with many litigation matters.

Another important and related development was the breakdown of the exclusive relationship that existed between many clients and their law firms. On those occasions when companies with house counsel need outside help, they usually look to more than one firm for such assistance. This breakdown of loyalty to one firm is attributable to several factors including the diverse employment backgrounds of the in-house lawyers, cost and service considerations, the desire to hire the best talent available, and the personal preferences and friendships of the in-house lawyers doing the hiring.

In any event, today it is unusual for a single outside firm to do all of the work of a major client or even all of the work done by outside counsel for such a client. It is the job of the inside general counsel and his or her staff to select outside counsel with the expertise and capability to assist with special jobs that cannot be covered by in-house staff. Consequently, it is more likely today that large companies, acting through their inside general counsel, will select several outside firms to assist in various aspects of their representation.

The changes over the thirty-five years ending in 1995 left the large business practice law firms in the United States in a different situation from where they had been in 1960. The lawyers in these firms are much better paid and generally less contented in their work. The firms are in fact very different organizations functioning in very different circumstances.

3 The Practice of Law in the 1990s

By the early 1990s the large law firms serving major business clients (most of which had been the major firms thirty years before) bore little resemblance to what they had been in the early 1960s. These 1990 behemoths were vastly larger, and they were more capable, aggressive, marketing-oriented, diverse, and profitable than they had been in 1960. Paradoxically, they were less influential in their communities, and their lawyers were not as happy with their work.

FIRM SIZE AND COMPOSITION

In 1995, 20 law firms in the United States employed over 500 lawyers, 151 employed over 200 lawyers, and at least another 100 firms employed over 125 lawyers. Most of the firms with over 200 lawyers had been among the relatively large firms in 1960. However, size is not always indicative of profitability. Wachtell, Lipton, Rosen & Katz, a New York firm with 109 lawyers in 1994, had the highest level of profits per partner.[1]

The largest firm based in the United States in 1995, Baker & McKenzie, had 1,754 lawyers, but only 449 were stationed in the United States. Its gross income in 1994 was $546 million. The second largest American firm and the one with the largest gross income ($582 million) was Skadden, Arps, Slate, Meagher & Flom with 1,119 lawyers (1,042 based in the United States). The third largest American firm but the one with the most U.S.- based lawyers was Jones, Day, Reavis & Pogue, which had 1,053 of its 1,118 lawyers stationed in the United States. Shearman, Sterling & Wright, the largest American firm in 1960 with 125 lawyers, would not have made the list of the 250 largest firms in 1995.

The largest business practice firm based in Atlanta in 1995 was still King & Spalding, employing 345 lawyers in Atlanta, Washington, New York, and Houston (136 partners, 178 associates, 25 counsel, and 6 staff attorneys). The second largest firm headquartered in Atlanta, Alston & Bird, had 308 lawyers (130 partners, 160 associates, and 18 counsel of various sorts), and offices in Atlanta, Washington, and Gwinnett County, Georgia. Sutherland, Asbill & Brennan had 275 lawyers (132 partners, 119 associates, and 24 counsel) and offices in Atlanta, Washington, New York, and Austin, Texas. The survival of Sutherland's New York office appeared in doubt in the fall of 1995 when 24 of the office's 25 lawyers announced plans to leave.[2] Powell Goldstein was the fourth in size with 226 lawyers (104 partners, 113 associates, and 9 counsel) and offices in Atlanta and Washington, D.C. Kilpatrick & Cody was the fifth in size with 210 lawyers (104 partners, 94 associates, and 12 counsel) and offices in Atlanta and Augusta, Georgia, Washington, London, and Brussels. The Kilpatrick firm added an Augusta office on January 1, 1994, in conjunction with the acquisition by merger of a health care and litigation firm that also had offices in Atlanta.

The firms' totals, however, do not always reflect their position in Atlanta alone. For instance, if only lawyers resident in Atlanta were counted, Alston & Bird (303 attorneys), would be ranked ahead of King & Spalding (246). Sutherland, Asbill, though ranked third in total lawyers, has traditionally been split between offices in Washington and Atlanta. In 1995, only 126 Sutherland attorneys were located in the Atlanta office. This figure is lower than Powell, Goldstein's (161 in Atlanta), Kilpatrick & Cody's (169 in Atlanta), or Troutman Sanders (182 in Atlanta). The Atlanta office of Jones, Day employed 90 of the 1,118 lawyers in the firm worldwide in 1995, or about 8 percent of the firm's total.[3]

The seven largest Atlanta law firms grew from 111 lawyers in 1960 to 1,643 lawyers in 1995.[4] Of these lawyers, 717 were identified as partners, 808 as associates, and the remainder were in a variety of counsel and staff attorney categories. As the partnerships grew in size, they also grew in complexity. Many firms created a new category of "nonequity partners" who receive a salary from the firm but do not participate in the firm's profits as partners with a percentage share. Some firms give these nonequity partners a formal vote in their affairs, and some do not. There were estimated to be 43 nonequity partners in 1993 in the seven large Atlanta firms; the number in previous years cannot readily be determined.[5] Of the 462 partners in 1990, 29 were women (6.2%) and 6 were African Americans. Of the 564 associates, 194 were women (slightly over a third) and 21 were African Americans.[6] In 1993 the seven firms reported a total of 10 black partners and 29 black associates.[7]

The extraordinary growth of the firms is even more remarkable when it is considered against the background of other developments in the profession. In the seventies and eighties, firms started hiring a large number of legal assistants (paralegals) who performed some of the work historically done by junior associates. At the same time, there was a significant increase in the number of lawyers being hired by businesses as full-time in-house employees to do work that had formerly been done by outside lawyers, including a lot of work previously done by associates.

So while legal assistants and in-house lawyers were taking over responsibility for much of the work that had traditionally been performed by junior associates, most of the large business practice firms were more than doubling in size each decade and more than doubling their number of associates and, in the process, increasing their associate leverage. The associate leverage configuration of the seven largest firms in Atlanta changed from 0.6 associates per partner in 1960, to 0.7 associates per partner in 1970, to slightly more than 1 associate per partner in 1980, to 1.3 associates per partner in 1990, before declining to 1.22 in 1995.[8] The associate leverage ratios of the major New York firms were high in 1960, and they remain high today. The ratio of associates per partner at Cravath, the second most profitable firm in the country in 1994, was over 3.62:1. The average associate leverage of the ten most profitable American law firms in 1994 was approximately 2.69:1.[9] However, associate leverage is not the only determinant of profitability. In 1994 Wachtell, Lipton, Rosen & Katz, the most profitable major business practice firm in America, had slightly less than one associate per partner.

The doubling of the associate leverage from 1960 to 1990 was one of the fundamental changes in the structure of the major business practice firms in Atlanta and throughout the nation, a change that has reshaped and transformed these institutions into entirely new creations. As the total number and percentage of inexperienced associates have increased, the average level of maturity and experience of major firm lawyers has inevitably declined and with it the quality and value of the firms' work product. The burden of recruiting, training, and supervising this growing army of inexperienced associates has weighed heavily on the shoulders of the more senior lawyers in the firms. An even greater burden on the senior lawyers has been the necessity of finding enough work suitable for these inexperienced lawyers to keep them sufficiently occupied to cover their high salaries.

It is one thing for a few select law firms to operate with significant associate leverage. It is quite another for hundreds of large law firms to operate in this manner. As will be discussed in chapter 10, the increase in the percentage of young and inexperienced lawyers doing the work of major law firms has affected the quality, nature, and cost of the legal products and services provided by these law firms.

SPECIALIZATION

Specialization has become the order of the day. At most firms, new associates are assigned to a department before they start to work, and they are expected to remain in that department until they retire. A lawyer's opportunity to become a partner is to a large extent dependent on the ages and numbers of partners already in the department and the growth in that area of the firm's practice.

Within the departments most lawyers have an area of subspecialization. Being a corporate finance lawyer or a litigator is no longer enough. You need a more sharply focused area of specialization such as mergers of financial institutions, or trials of product liability cases, or securities law claims, and many have an even narrower focus. More often than not with major corporate clients, partners are expected to be experts, and senior partners are expected to be at the peak of the expertise pyramid.

Specialization has been dictated by several considerations. In the first place, the body of the law has grown so much that it is no longer possible for even the brightest and hardest working lawyer to keep current with more than a small part of it. Billing expectations, competition, and rapid response requirements of clients do not permit the leisurely pursuit of knowledge that was practiced in the 1960s. In addition, the significant growth of in-house staff has greatly changed the nature of the outside legal services required. With in-house lawyers providing much of the general counseling of corporate officers and providing advice with respect to the recurring legal issues faced by their employers, outside counsel is normally expected to provide expertise with respect to unusual problems that do not occur every day or about which the in-house staff does not have expert knowledge. As a result, the demand has increased for experts and decreased for generalists. Many areas that did not appear likely to be taken over by in-house counsel twenty-five years ago have been taken in-house. Federal securities law compliance is one such example.

As the numbers and percentages of younger lawyers have increased, it has been necessary for these younger lawyers to develop specialized knowledge earlier in their careers in order for the firms to sell their services to clients and to justify their billing rates. All of these factors have contributed to the necessity of earlier specialization and more intensive specialization than in the past.

Most courts now require that lawyers who practice before them take continuing legal education courses in litigation-related subjects. If you have not taken these courses, you cannot appear in court. You cannot just go to court when the opportunity and the spirit move you.

MARKETING LEGAL SERVICES

The market for the services provided by the major business practice firms has become highly competitive. There are more good lawyers and law firms than there are clients and legal business available to outside firms. The "firm client" is largely a thing of the past. As a result, every major firm has a marketing program, and most have full-time nonlawyer personnel involved in that program. Numerous consultants sell marketing advice to these firms. Most large firms have retained public relations counsel to assist them in securing press coverage and in preparing promotional materials.

It is commonplace today for the major firms to pursue the business of companies represented by other law firms. Restrictions on such activities have vanished. The advent of house counsel has helped make marketing respectable. In-house general counsel are knowledgeable buyers of legal services. An important part of general counsel's role is to select firms that can provide required services for the best price.

Most general counsel are courted by outside firms more than they care to be. Firms send newsletters, books, and pamphlets they have prepared (or purchased from third-party providers with the firm's name on them) to promote their services, and they give free seminars on important developments in the law to which they invite not only their own clients but also executives and in-house lawyers who are clients of other law firms. Social events usually occur during or following these seminars at which the attendees are wined, dined, and pursued. These activities, which are directed to prospective clients, would have been a breach of the canons of ethics and grounds for discipline and perhaps disbarment thirty years ago.

Most lawyers have sought to market their services based on their expertise. They have sought to convince their clients that they have a higher level of knowledge and experience than the competition. In order to reach the users of legal services, lawyers join organizations and attend trade association meetings where potential clients gather. The trade associations themselves have become increasingly specialized, and as a result lawyers seeking to develop clients in these areas have had to shape their practice to correspond to the industry configuration.

Law firm marketing activity has become a burden to be borne by existing and potential clients, trade associations, and other organizations. It is often difficult to find the business members of these associations at meetings because of the multitude of lawyers and accountants in attendance. Some national associations now sponsor annual law and accounting conferences designed to attract lawyers and accountants and to introduce them to the company personnel focused on these issues.

The narrowing focus of marketing efforts has created a problem for many lawyers, especially for older lawyers who have developed several areas of special knowledge over their careers. There is a tendency to try to hang on to all of these areas of knowledge in the hope that a client in need of one or the other will call.

There is also a natural reluctance to give up an area of expertise in which there has been a significant investment over the years. On the other hand, such an effort can be both frustrating and futile. House counsel will often pass over a lawyer with broad general knowledge for someone who has concentrated in a narrow area and thus has developed a greater level of expertise and reputation. As a result, the older lawyer is often faced with the wrenching decision to forgo a portion of his invested professional capital to specialize in a particular area without the certainty that the business will be there to support him.

Younger lawyers face a similar problem in selecting or being led or forced into a narrow area of specialization from the very early days of their practice, without any way of knowing if their specialization will survive a forty-year career. Many lawyers find it difficult to live comfortably with this level of uncertainty and change.

MARKETING AND COMMUNITY SERVICE

Personal relationships remain an important part of the process of cultivating clients, but not as important as they used to be. In-house counsel do not have the time or desire to endure all of the cultivation attempted by private practice lawyers and firms. Lawyers are much more likely to be hired for what they know and can do than for whom they know.

One significant impact of restructuring in the profession has been to change the way lawyers participate in community affairs. Part of the reason for this change is the billable hour and client cultivation expectations of the law firms, which leave little time for community service or, for that matter, for family responsibilities.

Today, the largest percentage of legal work performed for large business clients is directed to outside lawyers by in-house counsel. In-house counsel most often are looking for particular legal knowledge or skills, and most are themselves judged by their

employers by the levels of success and the cost control achieved
by the lawyers they select.

Because lawyers are now permitted to brag about their expertise and experience, in-house counsel are provided with information to use in selecting law firms that is much more relevant than
the information gained from associating with lawyers in civic activity. In-house lawyers are working long hours themselves and
have less time to be involved in civic affairs. In any event, they are
not free, as top management sometimes is, to select the company's
lawyers on the basis of how they serve the community. As a result,
community service is less likely to generate new business today.

The fact that clients are less inclined to reward lawyers or law
firms for civic contributions has not been lost on the younger
generation of lawyers. Many younger lawyers, pressed by high billable hour expectations, spend little or no time on community service, and they see less potential benefit to themselves from undertaking it.

Nonetheless, large numbers of younger lawyers are involved in
community, not-for-profit service in Atlanta and in other communities around America, and they are much more involved than
they are given credit for. There has been a tremendous increase in
the number of minority and female lawyers over the last thirty
years and a resulting increase in such lawyers' involvement in
community affairs. This shift may account for some of the apparent decline in civic activity by white male lawyers.

However, there does appear to be a change in the leadership in
public affairs provided by lawyers, if not a change in the level of
involvement. The level of involvement necessary to provide leadership and the ability to manage one's time to provide leadership
have been affected by the increasing time demands of the large
firm practice and the reduced amount of energy available for
other things. I have also heard tales of lawyers no longer welcome
on the boards of directors of some cultural organizations because
of some lawyers' blatant efforts to use their positions to further
their legal practices.

There has also been a significant change in the status of lawyers in the community, a change which affects the community
leadership's view of the suitability of lawyers to lead major civic
organizations. The public's lack of admiration for lawyers in general is certainly a factor, too. Furthermore, as CEOs have hired
their own general counsel in-house, they have begun to think of
senior lawyers as underlings rather than as peers. The very label
"lawyer" draws rude jokes and denigrates the character of the person so labeled. Today those lawyers who rise to prominence in civic
affairs do so despite their profession rather than because of it.

When King & Spalding's John Sibley was drafted into the job of
chairman and president of the Trust Company of Georgia (the
Coca-Cola bank) in 1946, the move from senior partner to bank
president was viewed by many as a loss of status.[10] Such a response today would be unthinkable. In Atlanta between 1949 and
1957, two presidents of the chamber of commerce were prominent
senior partners in major local firms.[11] Over the past thirty-eight
years, the only lawyer to serve as chamber president has been former Georgia governor George Busbee, who was selected more for
his political standing than for his status as a lawyer. Although
many lawyers who entered the practice of law in the 1950s and
1960s are providing high-level leadership in Atlanta and in Georgia today, it is not obvious where their successors within their
firms are coming from.

INCREASING DIVERSITY AND
SOURCES OF LEGAL TALENT

In the early 1990s, most partners of the major Atlanta business
practice firms still came from middle- or upper-income homes.
There are now a significant number of women and a few African
American partners. The seven largest firms in Atlanta reported
1,081 lawyers in 1990, of whom 223 were women and 27 were African Americans. Although some firms had fewer black associates

than black partners, most had many more female associates than female partners. This reflects the tremendous increase in the number of women graduating from law school and the stagnation in the number of black graduates. Today, most law schools will lend enough money to needy students to enable them to complete school. As a result more people from economically disadvantaged circumstances are becoming lawyers.

Because of the extraordinary increase in beginning associate compensation, most new associates in 1995 are able to pay their expenses and live quite well. If married to another big-firm lawyer, as is often the case, they live extremely well. Buying a nice house, expensive foreign cars, and luxury vacations is a matter of course. However, many recent graduates have accumulated large loans to finance their college and law school educations, and servicing this debt has an effect on their financial circumstances.

The growth in the large business practice firms has not been matched by a growth in the elite sources of legal talent. The Harvard and Yale law schools have not increased the size of their student bodies in thirty years. The number of students on the *Harvard Law Review* each year is approximately the same now as in 1960. As a result, as the large business practice firms have grown, they have had to change their standards with respect to the credentials of students they hire. Competition for top students is intense. All large business practice firms are recruiting in the national job market and have to respond to salaries paid in New York City, Chicago, or Los Angeles.

SUPPORT STAFF

The large firms today all have sizable staffs of nonlawyer personnel to assist in operation and management. The cost of this staff is one of the factors driving up the cost of legal services. The single largest part of the nonlawyer staff continues to be legal secretaries. This is a very demanding job requiring the skills normally associated with an "executive assistant" plus the ability to produce large quantities of flawlessly typed material. Firms have been seeking to reduce the secretary-lawyer ratio by increasing secretarial efficiency and thereby reducing costs. Despite the increased productivity brought about by computerized word processing and laser printers, firms have made less progress in reducing the number of secretaries than they had expected. Although the ratios have fallen some since the early 1980s, as lawyers have put in longer hours there has inevitably been more for their secretaries to do. As lawyers themselves have become proficient at producing their own documents on computerized word processing systems, firms are beginning to see some of the increased productivity that was anticipated twenty years ago.

Legal assistant (paralegal) has become an important job category that did not formally exist in 1960, although many of the best legal secretaries functioned in this role. By establishing a legal assistant category, the firms created another category of time billers and as a result were able to recover a fee for some work formerly performed by secretaries without charge. Legal assistants also do at a lower hourly charge work formerly done by lawyers. During my first several years of practice, I organized many corporations, processed U.S. and foreign trademark applications, and answered garnishments. This type of work today would most often be handled by a legal assistant in a large business practice firm, or it would be done in-house.

Numerous people are involved in opening, storing, and retrieving files. Computer experts manage the firm's word processing, document preservation, computer network, and internal time and finance records. Bookkeepers and accountants keep track of bills to clients for legal services and disbursements, receivables, and payables. There are facilities maintenance and supply personnel and food and beverage service personnel. Copying facilities for most large firms are the equivalent of print shops, and we find marketing personnel, fringe benefit administrators, personnel supervisors, et cetera.

Most large firms have a staff of librarians who manage the firms' library resources, are familiar with electronic databases and with resources available in other public and law firm libraries, and can arrange access to these materials for their lawyers.

TECHNOLOGY

There has been a tremendous increase in the amount of technology available to expedite the provision of legal services. Copying machines, fax machines, cellular phones, pagers, computerized word processors, document production systems, computerized legal research, and voice mail have made lawyers more accessible to their clients. As a result, lawyers are expected to respond more quickly to clients' needs.

Technology has also had the effect of removing barriers that formerly protected lawyers from client demands. Clients today often expect a document to be produced immediately upon request and to be completed promptly by the exchange of faxed revisions until the job is done. A lawyer can no longer drop a draft document into the mail and expect a respite of several days during which he or she can work on other matters. Client expectations have increased, and in the process the pressures brought to bear on lawyers have also increased.

We enjoy vastly greater sources of information. Thirty years ago, lawyers relied primarily on statutes, published regulations, and case law to advise clients. Today, we use numerous secondary sources including textbooks, newsletters, and specialized services. There is electronic research capability such as LEXIS, WestLaw, and Information America.

THE HIGHER RISKS OF PURSUING A LEGAL EDUCATION

Law schools jumped on the higher compensation bandwagon during the last thirty-five years by increasing their tuition charges substantially in excess of inflation, and students have borrowed heavily to pay the higher costs (tuition at the Harvard Law School has increased from $1,250 a year in 1961 – 62 to $17,750 in 1993 – 94, an increase of 1,320 percent). Large loans have been justified on the grounds that highly compensated young lawyers could afford to pay them back. The availability of loans to pay most of one's law school expenses had the desirable effect of opening law school to many minority and other candidates who could not have afforded law school without the expansion of the loan program. It has also opened law school to many students whose families were reluctant to spend their disposable income on a legal education for their children. However, the detrimental effects of the easy availability of law school loans have been significant.

Many students also borrow money through government loans to attend college. These loans become due for initial payments six months after graduation (or after dropping out, if a student does not graduate). As a result, such college graduates have an incentive to stay in school, particularly if jobs are scarce upon graduation. Many have chosen to attend law school in order to postpone the payment of college loans and in the hope of finding jobs that pay well enough to service both their undergraduate and law school educational debt. Many students today finish law school owing as much as $80,000, and many have college-related debt of an equal amount. They need high-paying jobs to pay it back. The need to repay these loans when the borrowers' schooling is complete has replaced student deferments from military service as a principal incentive for new college graduates to enroll immediately in law school. Because law schools can charge a high tuition and have low faculty-to-student ratios, they are often profitable to their universities, and these profits are used to support other university academic programs.

An unfortunate feature of this loan program is that students cannot take time off after college or during law school to earn money to pay for their education, or to think about their futures, without accelerating the due date of their college and law school debt. It is a disaster for those law students who cannot find high-paying jobs upon graduation. The ease of acquiring the loans is, unfortunately, also an inducement to a student pursuing an ill-advised legal career when it is unlikely that the student will finish high enough in his or her class to get one of the highly compensated jobs that make it possible to pay off the loans.

A surprising number of students attend law school because they cannot find jobs that suit them and cannot think of anything else they would prefer to do. A legal education has the advantage of enhancing a person's analytical and presentation skills, which are useful in almost any occupation. In addition, there is a substantial overlap between a graduate business school program and a legal education. Consequently, many law school graduates become business persons rather than lawyers, or they switch later in their careers. Some students pursue joint degree programs in both business and law. In any event, the large number of students who drift into law school because they cannot find something else they would prefer to do contributes to the unusually high level of law graduates who ultimately are dissatisfied with the practice of law.

THIRTY YEARS OF CHANGE

By the early 1990s the life of the major business practice lawyer had become much more demanding and complex. The advantage of very high pay has been offset by longer hours, more responsibility, more client pressure, and greater insecurity. Those young lawyers working for firms below the top rung often find lower pay, hours as long as if they had been making $60,000 a year, greater competition for clients, and even greater insecurity.

The major business practice firm of the 1990s is a mixed blessing to its partners, associates, and other personnel, as well as to its clients. Lawyers at all levels are much better compensated in real dollars than they were thirty years ago. Chapter 4 will look more closely at the evolution of large-firm lawyer compensation, and chapter 5 will examine working conditions in the 1990s.

4 Compensation

The extraordinary increase in major firm lawyer compensation at all levels is one of the most important changes that has occurred in the legal profession over the last thirty years. The effort to maintain and increase this extraordinary compensation has been one of the driving forces in the transformation of the practice of law during the last twenty years.

ASSOCIATE COMPENSATION

In 1960 most new associates in Atlanta fresh from law school earned $3,600 a year. At the Alston firm, an unmarried associate was paid only $3,300. Associates' starting salaries increased to $4,800 in 1961, and to $6,000 in 1962. The Kilpatrick firm paid a $100 monthly premium over the other firms until 1962. The increase in starting pay of 66 percent over a three-year period from 1960 to 1962 represented an extraordinary jump.

Starting salaries then advanced to $6,200 in 1963, $6,300 in 1964, $7,200 in 1965, $8,400 in 1967, $10,800 in 1968, and to $14,000 in 1969, the level at which they remained until 1974. Starting salaries had increased 289 percent in a decade in which inflation had been 24 percent. These increases occurred in part because Atlanta firms were entering the national job market and actively recruiting at national law schools and because of the growing demand for legal services, which was increasing the national competition for the best students. New York and Washington, D.C., could no longer take for granted that most law review graduates of the national schools would at least want to begin their careers there.

The Vietnam War played a special role in the escalation of associate compensation. When student deferments were abolished in 1966, law school enrollment shrank slightly at the same time that many students graduating from law school were required to enter military service. As a result, the available supply of graduates was low in 1967 at a time when the demand for associates was increasing.

At least partly in response to this pressure, Cravath Swaine & Moore of New York City announced in 1968 the first of its infamous raises of starting salaries with a jump from approximately $10,500 a year to $15,000. This move profoundly shocked the entire legal community. Every firm in the national job market had to decide how they would respond to the Cravath initiative. At this point the competitive instincts and pride of the major firms came into play.

The large firms in New York responded by matching the Cravath initiative, and the compensation race was on. Each firm felt it was as good as Cravath or at least in the same league. To pay a lower starting salary would appear to be an admission of weak-

ness – either an inability to match the Cravath salary or a mean-
ness of spirit resulting in an unwillingness to do so.

Cravath and other major firms continued the established practice of paying all starting associates the same salary regardless of
their academic achievements and personal qualifications. The compensation of most senior associates usually increased at the same
time as the starting salaries increased but not always or uniformly
in the same amount. Even if the dollar amount of the raise in starting salaries was also given to all of the other associates (often it
was not), the increase represented a smaller percentage increase
for the more highly paid senior associates than for the beginners.

The response of other business practice firms throughout the
country to the Cravath initiative depended to a large extent on
whether or not they were recruiting students at the national law
schools. If they were, they generally felt that they had to respond
to the Cravath initiative by raising their own starting salaries substantially. Because of cost-of-living differentials and other advantages, the major Atlanta firms did not feel that they had to pay the
same salary as Cravath. They raised their starting salaries from
$8,400 in 1967 to $10,800 in 1968, and to $14,000 in 1969. Cra-
vath and its New York competition also continued to raise theirs.

Although firms in other cities have rarely matched New York
salaries, those in the national job market cannot ignore them. As
a result, salaries went up in all cities that competed in that market.
Atlanta firms were among the few from southern cities that re-
cruited at the national law schools. In many other cities where
there was a slower rate of growth, prominent law firms could still
attract a few of the best students from the local university law
schools who wanted to remain in the vicinity, and as a result such
firms could meet their growth needs without paying competitive
national rates. Beginning in the late sixties, Atlanta firms found
themselves most often competing with firms in Dallas, Houston,
Washington, San Francisco, Los Angeles, and Denver.

The tremendous increase in demand for new lawyers that drove
up compensation by more than 65 percent in two years (from
$8,400 in 1967 to $14,000 in 1969) is also seen in the extraordinary

increase in the number of students attending law school in the late 1960s. Law school enrollment of first-year students increased from 24,000 in school year 1967 – 68 to 36,000 in school year 1971 – 72, an increase of 50 percent over four years. These two facts, more than any others, prove just how much the demand for lawyers was increasing across the nation. The actual availability of new lawyers to the firms lagged behind this curve by three years, so the increased supply (augmented further by the release of lawyers from the military services where some functioned as lawyers but many more as soldiers) did not begin to reach the firms until the fall of 1972. By 1980, new associate compensation had increased to $24,000 a year, an increase of $10,000 (or 71 percent) during the seventies when inflation had been 98 percent.

In the late seventies and early eighties, as the number and percentage of associates increased, the percentage of those making partner declined, the required working hours grew longer, and the years of service as an associate were extended. These changes made the practice of law at the major firms less attractive. In addition, although the demand for new associates increased in the 1980s, total law school enrollment barely changed. Total national enrollment in the J.D. program was 119,501 in academic year 1980 – 81, and it was 120,694 in 1988 – 89. However, the number of female students increased from 40,834 in 1980 – 81 to 50,932 in 1988 – 89, with a corresponding drop in the number of male students enrolled from 78,667 to 69,762.[1] Although I do not know of any studies of the issue, I believe that there may have remained a lingering preference for hiring male associates, who were in much shorter supply, which may have been a factor in the willingness of law firms to push up starting salaries.

In any event, during the 1980s, with demand at an all-time high and the supply of new associates static (or, with respect to male prospects, shrinking by approximately 12 percent), the law firms responded as they had in the 1960s: they raised starting salaries dramatically. This phenomenon was also fueled by competition from investment banking and major consulting firms, which began to offer astonishing salaries and benefits to attract top law school graduates.

During the 1980s, beginning associate compensation in Atlanta increased 150 percent, from $24,000 a year to $60,000. Inflation during the decade was 71 percent. Salaries increased to even higher levels in many other major cities. The starting salary at major business practice firms in New York in 1990 was $83,000. Cravath again took the lead in escalating salaries by raising its starting salary from $53,000 to $65,000 in 1986.[2]

Just as they did between 1969 and 1974, beginning salaries in Atlanta remained unchanged from 1990 until the fall of 1996, when the major Atlanta firms raised their starting salaries to $67,000. Starting salaries at most of the major New York firms have now crept up to $85,000. The Atlanta firms realized that they had raised their salaries higher than necessary to attract the talent they needed in the early 1990s as the demand for their services stagnated or declined and the supply of law graduates began to increase. (Total enrollment in J.D. programs increased from 120,694 in 1988 – 89 to 128,989 in 1994 – 95.) However, the damage had already been done.

Starting associate compensation at major law firms in Atlanta rose from $3,600 a year in 1960 to $60,000 in 1990, an increase of 1,567 percent versus inflation of 339 percent. Had starting salaries been increased only for inflation since 1960, they would have been about $15,000 in 1990. Had starting salaries been increased only for inflation from their 1980 level of $24,000, they would have been about $41,000 in 1990.

First-year associate salaries from 1960 to 1995 are set forth in Figure 4.1. For comparison, the lower line represents what salaries would have been if they had been adjusted annually for inflation, starting from the base year of 1960.

PARTNER COMPENSATION
THE 1960S

In Atlanta in 1960, first-year partners in some major firms earned as little as $18,000 and in others they earned as much as

FIGURE 4.1 ACTUAL ASSOCIATE COMPENSATION IN ATLANTA
VERSUS INFLATION-ADJUSTED COMPENSATION, 1960–1995

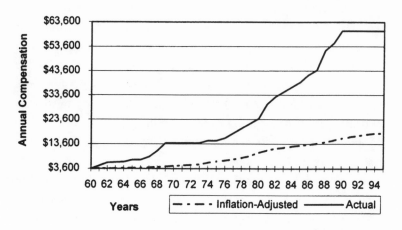

$41,000, but most earned around $20,000. The average partner's earnings ranged from $23,000 to $59,000 or more, and the highest paid partners in the same firms earned as little as $45,000 or as much as $93,000 a year.[3] Only one earned as much as $93,000, and he did not fare as well the following year. Most of the highest paid partners earned substantially less.

Starting in the early sixties, as associate leverage began to increase, partner compensation rose in excess of the rate of inflation. By 1970, first-year partners in several major Atlanta firms were earning $30,000 to $41,000 a year or more. The average partners were earning $59,000 to $80,000 or more, and the highest paid partners were earning in a range of $90,000 to $142,000 or more, depending on the firm. Starting partner income had increased by 67 percent at the low end of the scale, whereas the upper end had remained stable. By 1970, average partner income at the low end of the range had increased 160 percent and the top end had increased 36 percent. The highest partner income had doubled at the low end, and the high end had increased by 53 percent. Inflation for the 1960s was 24 percent. Although significant differences between the high end and the low end of the scale continued to exist, these differences narrowed considerably as the firms at the low end gained ground on their competitors at the most highly compensated firms.

The more modest advance of new partner compensation reflected the strength of the firms and their senior partners in controlling the firm's business and the fact that new partners tended to compare their status more with the senior associate ranks from which they had recently departed than with senior partner compensation. There was no public information about the compensation paid in the various firms, and there was little speculation about it. New partners were interested in getting a raise in take-home pay after paying their capital contributions and the other expenses that they now had to cover for themselves but that were paid by the firm for associates. New partners were not told what senior partners earned, and if they asked, they might not find out. At the Alston firm the financial partner (one of the name partners) carried a list of partner compensation in his inside coat pocket. Any partner could ask to see the list, but it took some courage to do so. It took a good deal more to copy it down.

During the 1960s greater business activity and associate leverage produced a significant increase in profits for the firms' partners, with the more senior partners benefiting the most.

THE 1970S

Partner compensation failed to keep pace with inflation despite increased associate leverage and recorded hours. Starting partners in 1980 were earning $58,000 to $65,000 a year or more, average partners $96,000 to $105,000, and the highest paid partners $155,000 to $170,000 or more. New partner income had increased by 93 percent at the bottom end of the scale and 60 percent at the top; average partner income had risen 63 percent at the bottom and 31 percent at the top. The income of the highest paid partners increased by 72 percent at the bottom and 20 percent at the top, all in a decade in which inflation had been 98 percent.

During the late 1970s partners' compensation at most firms

and at most levels lost ground to inflation, as did that of associates. The range of differences in compensation among the firms followed the pattern of the 1960s and continued to decrease. The relatively greater increase in starting partner compensation reflected the fact that the firms had increased the number of years an associate had to serve before becoming a partner. Because of the longer time-in-grade, senior associate compensation was higher before becoming a partner, and a higher starting partner compensation was necessary if new partners were to get a raise.

The increase in starting partner compensation also reflected the growing strength of younger partners who for the first time had the power to control important clients. When firms grew in the late sixties and early seventies, the senior partners were generally busy looking after the needs of the firm's long-standing clients for whom they worked. As new clients came to the firm, they often became the responsibility of younger partners who had time available to devote to their needs. These newer clients often bonded with the younger partners and considered themselves clients of the lawyers rather than of the firm. As a result, some younger partners had the capacity to take substantial clients with them if they decided to move to another firm or to start their own. The inducement for making such a move was usually a significant increase in pay for the person who moved. Because the courts have looked with disfavor on noncompete agreements between law firms and their lawyers, compensation became the principal way of addressing this problem. To deter such moves, the firms found it necessary to raise the salaries of younger partners who controlled important client relationships.

THE 1980s
Inflation rose rapidly between 1979 and 1982, increasing more than 10 percent a year for three consecutive years. These inflationary years conditioned clients to accept the substantial rate increases that were necessary to offset inflation during that period. When inflation subsided by the mid-1980s, law firms were able to continue to increase their rates substantially without significant

client objection. Billing rates increased in excess of the rate of inflation; by 1989, billing rates had recaptured historic shortfalls and equaled or exceeded what they would have been had they increased with inflation since 1960. With hourly rates advancing more rapidly than inflation, total recorded and billed hours continuing to increase as partners and associates alike were pushed to increase their recording of billable time, and associate leverage at an all-time high, profits skyrocketed.

By 1990, new partners in Atlanta advancing from the associates ranks could expect to earn not less than $135,000, and in some firms they received at least $150,000, an increase of over 130 percent from 1980. Average partner compensation ranged from $259,000 to $395,000, an increase of 170 percent at the bottom end of the scale and 275 percent at the top. The highest paid partners were generally earning $475,000 to $600,000, an increase of over 200 percent at the low end and 250 percent at the high end, for a decade in which inflation had been 71 percent.

THE 1990S

Although average partner compensation in New York declined between 1988, which was the high-water mark of law firm profitability in New York, and 1995, average partner income in Atlanta continued to increase in the 1990s, in some cases to an extraordinary extent. For example, King & Spalding's average partner income in 1994 was reported to be $460,000, and Alston & Bird's was reported to be $435,000, up from $392,000 and $286,000, respectively, in 1990. The profits per partner of the major Atlanta firms were larger in 1994 than in 1988.[1]

Of the ten most profitable major business practice firms in America in 1988, not one reported profits as high per partner in 1994 as they had reported in 1988. However, of the top ten in 1988, eight remained in the top ten in 1994, reflecting a remarkable degree of consistency and good management.

Although no one will feel sorry for them, the decline for many firms was significant. The profits per partner at Cravath declined from $1,765,000 in 1988 to $1,225,000 in 1994 (31%). The profits per partner at Cahill Gordon & Reindel declined from $1,515,000 to $1,200,000 (21%), and at Skadden, Arps from $1,195,000 to $820,000 (32%). Hardest hit was the ninth-ranked firm in profitability in 1988: Fried, Frank, Harris, Shriver & Jacobson, whose profits per partner dropped from $815,000 to $400,000 in 1994 (51%) as the firm fell to the forty-ninth position on the profits per partner list. On the other hand, some major firms in New York were able to increase their profits per partner. Cleary, Gottlieb, Steen & Hamilton moved up from thirteenth position in 1988 to seventh in 1994 by increasing its profits per partner from $775,000 in 1988 to $885,000 in 1994. Debevoise & Plimpton moved from eighteenth on the list in 1988 to ninth by increasing its profits per partner from $655,000 to $805,000. The four firms that consistently generated profits per partner of over $1 million a year were Cravath, Swaine & Moore; Wachtell, Lipton, Rosen & Katz; Cahill Gordon & Reindel; and Sullivan & Cromwell.[5]

The range of beginning partner compensation in Atlanta between 1960 and 1990 increased in inflation-adjusted dollars by 79 percent at the bottom end and showed a decline of 12 percent at the top end. There had been very few beginning partners at the top end in 1960. The increase in average partner compensation in Atlanta from its 1960 range of $23,000 to $59,000 to a range of $259,000 to $392,000 in 1990 represented an increase in inflation-adjusted dollars ranging from 170 percent at the low end to 60 percent at the high end. The range of highest paid partner compensation increased in inflation-adjusted dollars by 153 percent at the bottom and 54 percent at the top.

The degree of increase in the compensation of the most highly paid partners depended a lot on their particular firms. At one of the major Atlanta firms, the compensation of the highest paid partner in 1960 had been about $45,000, and his 1994 successor in interest earned approximately $550,000, representing an increase in inflation-adjusted dollars of 176 percent. At another major firm, the senior partner in 1960 earned $93,000 compared with his 1994 successor's income of $575,000, only a 40 percent

FIGURE 4.2 ACTUAL PARTNER COMPENSATION IN
ATLANTA AND AS ADJUSTED FOR INFLATION, 1960–1994

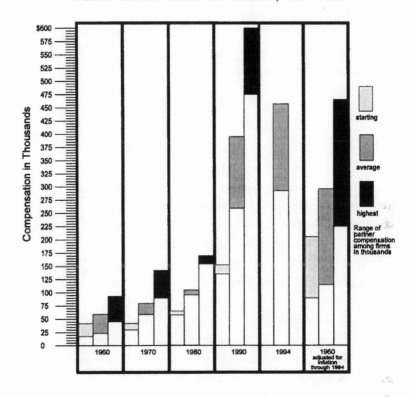

increase in inflation-adjusted dollars. One reason the income of partners with top compensation in the 1990s did not grow more is the fact that they were so much better paid earlier in their careers.

In the 1990s, partners at every level of practice in the major firms in Atlanta were much better paid in inflation-adjusted dollars than their predecessors thirty years before. Figure 4.2 illustrates the range of actual partner compensation and what such compensation would have been if it had merely been adjusted for inflation since 1960.

The increases in average partner income and highest-paid partner income adjusted for inflation over thirty-five years are significant. Per partner profits in 1960 adjusted for inflation would range from $115,000 to $296,000 compared with an actual range for all six firms in 1994 of $293,000 to $457,000. These numbers are all the more impressive in light of the decline in the average age of the partners in these firms so that these higher levels of income are generally being realized at an earlier age. In addition, only one or two senior partners in each firm were earning at the top levels of income in 1960, and there are many who do so today.

HOW WELL PAID ARE THE PARTNERS?

Big firm lawyers often seek to justify their own lofty compensation by the fact that the chief executive officers of their firms' major clients earn more than many partners in their firms. It should not be necessary to remind these partners that most of them are not the chief executive officer of anything, that their average earnings exceed the average earnings of senior executive officers in all but a handful of companies, and that their average age is a good deal lower than that of most executive officers.

Those lawyers who try to justify their large incomes by comparison with the high compensation typically paid to high-ranking executives of America's largest corporations are fishing for support in the wrong pond. Although business leaders in the highest echelon do indeed receive extremely high salaries and other compensation, outstripping all but the most exceptional business attorneys, the pay rate decreases sharply as one descends the corporate ladder.

Even a cursory survey of proxy statements proves the point. Federal disclosure laws require that the proxy statements of major public corporations reveal the compensation of the company's CEO and the next four highest paid officers. From one sample of large and prestigious corporations,[6] it appears that the annual compensation paid to the most highly paid executive declines on average by 58 percent when you reach the fifth most highly paid manager. The average annual compensation paid to the fifth-ranking executives in the sample is $587,000,[7] a sum exceeded by the profits per partner of sixteen of the firms on the "Am Law 100" survey for 1994.

Moreover, the characteristics of profit distribution in law firms are different from the steeply inclining salaries paid to the corporate managers. In our sample of companies, note that the compensation earned by the most highly paid executive was, on average, 2.5 times the compensation received by the fifth most highly paid person. It is apparent that large firm average partner income, though lower than that of the top executives at American corporations, is shared among a much larger and younger class of participants. It is not necessary to delve deeply into the corporate hierarchy before management compensation drops steeply below the average income of the partners in large law firms. As smaller companies are examined, we find that large-firm partner compensation is not insubstantial compared with that of business executives.

Indeed, it is difficult to see how major firm partner compensation could be deemed low by any objective standard. In the 1995 "Am Law 100" survey of the *American Lawyer*, the first fifty firms ranked by average partner profits had 6,065 partners and ranged in size from 55 to 500 partners (an average of 121), with average per partner profits ranging from $400,000 to $1.4 million. Of thirty large firms representing diverse geographic areas from a survey of annual attorney compensation, average partner profits were $310,000 distributed among an average class of 113 partners.[8]

Many more lawyers are partners in major firms today than in 1960 and many of them are exceptional people. However, most could not provide the leadership required by a major organization. They have created value for themselves in their law firms, but they are not creating value for others as is the case of many corporate executives building wealth for their shareholders. Not all of these partners were Phi Beta Kappas in college, nor did they all score in the 95th percentile or above on the law school aptitude test; they were not all at the top of their law school classes, and they were not all editors of their law reviews at quality law schools. Nonetheless, most expect to earn an annual income by

the time they are forty-five in the range of $250,000 to $350,000.[9]
The services that many of these individuals provide are not exceptional in terms of intellectual content or creativity. Much of
the work involves copying and modifying forms or prior documents, much of which is done without a great deal of imagination.
I believe that the best lawyers in the big firms are entitled to a
high level of income, but it is harder to justify the extraordinary
income drawn by the average partners in the larger firms.

THE IMPACT OF HIGHER COMPENSATION

There is little room to argue about the wisdom and necessity of
raising associate salaries to the extent they were raised in the sixties and seventies. The salaries in 1960 were very low by any reasonable standard. The Vietnam War created a short-term shortage
at a time of growing demand that contributed to the big increases
in the late sixties.

Also a factor was New York's fading popularity with law graduates in the late sixties and early seventies. As the size and quality
of firms in other cities grew, they were able to offer practice opportunities that rivaled those offered by the New York firms, with
better working conditions, better prospects for partnership, better
living conditions, and significantly increased compensation. As a
result, a large number of top-quarter graduates from national law
schools, who once would have interviewed in New York, did not
bother to do so. In response, most of the major New York firms
continued to push up their salaries, and for a few years they reduced their time to partnership and increased the percentage of
associates who became partners. This in turn put salary pressures
on their competitors in the major regional legal centers.

However, there is room to debate the wisdom of the ill-con-
ceived salary escalations of the 1980s from $24,000 to $60,000 a
year. The increase of associate starting compensation by 150 percent was unwise. Inflation during this period was 71 percent. Had

the 1980 starting salary been increased only for inflation, it would have been about $41,000 in 1990. Starting hourly billing rates went from $45 to a range of $80 to $90 – an increase of about 90 percent.

With associates already working longer and harder than normal human beings can work effectively, it should not come as a surprise that profitability per new associate shrank in real dollars. An associate billing 1,900 hours in 1980 at a rate of $45 an hour (assuming a 90 percent billed and collected rate) produced a profit of $52,950 before overhead allocation but after subtracting a salary of $24,000. The same associate in 1990, working the same hours at a rate of $80 an hour with the same billed and collected rate, but with a $60,000 salary, produced a profit of $76,800. In order to keep pace with inflation for the decade, the firm needed a gross profit on our hypothetical starting associate of $90,545, assuming that overhead had not increased in excess of inflation, which in fact I think it did. Profit per associate in real dollars declined during the eighties.

A decline in profit would normally have reduced the profits of law firm partners. Instead, partners' profits continued to increase in Atlanta during the 1980s from an average partner profit in the range of $96,000 to $105,000 in 1980 to a range of $259,000 to $395,000 in 1990, or an increase in inflation-adjusted dollars of approximately 170 percent at the low end of the scale to 276 percent at the high end. How could this happen?

The law firms were able to increase their profitability in the face of this trend because they were busy increasing their leverage and billable time and increasing their billing rates in excess of inflation, especially at the partner level. In the process, real cost to clients increased because of (1) higher lawyer compensation, (2) changes in the way legal services were delivered, which utilized larger numbers and percentages of associates, (3) increased billable time devoted to the client's business, and (4) billing rates that increased in excess of inflation. The result has been a decrease in the value of legal services provided by major business practice firms relative to the cost, an increase in the relative cost advantage of in-house counsel, and a serious deterioration of the competitiveness of private practice firms.

When starting salaries were raised to $60,000 a year in Atlanta in 1990 ($83,000 in New York), for the first time corporate clients could pay their in-house lawyers less than law firms paid and still attract a large number of excellent attorneys. The 150 percent increase in the compensation of law firm associates was much more than necessary to provide a very attractive lifestyle. Consequently, it was possible for companies to pay their in-house lawyers less than law firm lawyers earned but more than enough for their in-house lawyers to live very comfortably and pay off their student loans. This was different from 1960, when law firm associates could barely live on what they were paid and it was almost impossible to hire anyone to work in-house for less.

Taking into account some of the other advantages of in-house practice, such as not having to compete for clients, better control over working hours, and, in many cases, more humane work requirements, the relative attractiveness of in-house work skyrocketed, and many more good lawyers became interested in taking these jobs. As the number of highly competent in-house staff has grown, the need for outside legal services has been less than it otherwise would have been. During the same period, the concept of the in-house general counsel has evolved from a role as liaison with and supervisor of outside lawyers to the position of an accomplished leader of both an in-house law department and outside lawyers. In the process, the in-house general counsel often has replaced the outside general counsel and become the client's chief legal adviser. The changed role and the greatly increased importance of the in-house general counsel's job is reflected in compensation that often ranges from $400,000 to $600,000 and in a few cases is as high as $2 million a year.[10]

The large private practice firms, by recklessly increasing the compensation of their lawyers, by changing the way legal services are delivered to utilize too many inexperienced lawyers, and by pressing all lawyers to bill more time, have put the private bar at a significant cost disadvantage and have made possible the closing of the quality gap between in-house and outside lawyers. The combination has had a devastating effect on the relative advantage of outside versus inside counsel.

Many major firms, fortified by the ample egos that have sustained them for so long, deny the truth of this reality. But those of us who know the quality of in-house counsel at many of the country's major corporations also know that the quality advantage of outside counsel has diminished considerably if not entirely. In addition, the practical and responsive way in which many in-house lawyers are able to respond to the legal needs of their employer-clients is a more cost-effective way of delivering legal services than the styles adopted by many of the major firms.

Unfortunately for the major-firm partners, associate compensation is not the most important factor causing the cost disadvantage of outside counsel. Assume for a moment that starting associate compensation in Atlanta were reduced from $60,000 to $40,000 a year — a 33 percent reduction and about where it would have been had it been increased for inflation in the eighties — with fringe benefits remaining unchanged. Assume further that billable hour expectations were reduced from 1,900 hours to 1,700 hours — about 11 percent — to partially offset the reduction in pay. The compensation received by the associate for each billable hour would drop by $8 an hour — from approximately $31.50 an hour to $23.50 per hour. If all of these savings were passed on to clients, it would reduce the associate's starting billable rate from $85 an hour to $77, for a reduction of 9.4 percent.

Why this disparity? Why doesn't a 33 percent reduction in pay result in a 33 percent reduction in costs to clients for associate services? In the first place, the other overhead items in the firm's operations, from rent to secretarial salaries, would remain unchanged. In the second place, and of greater importance, the firm would not have reduced its profit (that is, the amount going to the partners for each associate hour billed).

The $53.50 difference between the billable hourly rate and the associate's cash compensation remains the same in either scenario.

A portion pays the overhead, and a portion goes to partners' profits. Unless the firm's landlord or support staff can be persuaded to participate in a cost-reduction program, the only place greater reductions can occur is in partner profit. Even if billable hour expectations were kept at 1,900 hours, rather than reduced to partially offset the drop in salary, the savings to clients in the reduction of associate billable rates by 33 percent would be only about 12 percent.

It is a mistake to assume that the difference between what a corporation pays a young lawyer in salary and what is paid to the young lawyers by a private practice firm is the measure of the cost savings of in-house counsel. The larger saving comes from the elimination of the partner profit on the associates' work.

Is the partner profit from associate work justified? That depends on whether or not the partners are able to increase the value of their associates' labors by the training and guidance the associates receive from the partners, and whether or not the value they add in that process is greater than the value that would be added by the training and supervision of senior in-house lawyers.

Another way of looking at the question is to ask whether the knowledge and skill of the partner is so great that the client is willing to pay an excessive rate for the partner's associates to assist him on the matter even though to do so drives up the client's costs. Compared with other alternatives, is the value of the partner's services equal to the total cost of receiving the service from him, including the profit he makes from the charges for the other lawyers working with him on the matter?

For example, if the partner's billing rate is $300 an hour and the rate of the associate working with him is $120 an hour and the project requires ten hours of work from the partner and thirty from the associate, the cost to the client will be $6,600. If the associate works 1,900 billable hours and earns $72,000 a year, the associate is paid $37.90 an hour plus the cost of benefits. Assuming the cost of those benefits and of the associate's share of overhead is $68.42 an hour (an arbitrary figure), the firm makes a $14 an hour profit on the associate's time. If the work were done in-house with a senior lawyer and a lawyer three or four years out of law school, the company would at least save the $14 an hour associate profit or $420 on the cost of the project by doing it in-house. In addition, the hourly cost of the legal services of the in-house senior lawyer is generally much less than the cost of purchasing such hours from a senior partner of a major firm.

Most major law firms have ignored the fact that as the ratio of associates to partners has increased, the partners' ability to add value to each associate working under their supervision has decreased. In many large firms, associates work without significant partner supervision because the partners do not have the time to provide it. It is equally true that the value to a client of using the services of a particular partner may be eroded by the cost of involving other lawyers in his firm on the project, especially when there are less expensive options for achieving the same result. Clients are now asking themselves such questions, and law firms that wish to survive and prosper will need to find good answers.

A key issue in law practice economics in the years ahead will be the extent to which partners can justify their firm's associate leverage by working as hard as necessary to do so. This is a more difficult issue for the firms than the prices they charge for their partners' time.

Many of today's associates and younger partners were attracted to the profession by the prospect of superior compensation. Many of them, especially the most compulsive, feel entitled to these high levels of compensation. They will not willingly surrender the compensation they expected when they entered law school.

On the other hand, historical compensation data over the past thirty-five years makes it clear that large-firm lawyers have not always been as well paid in real dollars as they are today. Their high level of compensation is an important factor in the high cost to clients. Larger clients and many smaller ones are responding by restructuring their relationships with their outside lawyers and by making efforts to get more out of their in-house staffs. I think it is highly unlikely that clients will continue to contribute gladly to their outside law firms' extraordinary profitability feast. I do think it is highly likely that clients will continue to work to reduce major firm revenues by demanding more cost-effective service, that the firms will be forced to respond, and that their partners will be forced to live with lower but still generous incomes or to become more cost-effective lawyers, and perhaps both.

5 Working Conditions

Among the defining characteristics of the practice of law in major business firms is a high level of stress. The principal contributing factors are long hours; multiple simultaneous projects; demanding requirements of accuracy, precision, punctuality, and response; and the large amounts of profit or loss involved in the work. To these pressures are often added prima donna bosses (lawyers and clients) highly motivated by success and money. Of course, conditions vary from firm to firm, from job to job, and within firms.

THE OVERWORKED LAWYER

It is clear that in the early sixties most firms in Atlanta did not keep track of time by individual lawyer. Most lawyers were expected to put in a full day's work five days a week and a half day or more on Saturday several weekends a month. For a period of years continuing into the late 1970s, the Alston firm did not look at the billable time of individual lawyers. As chairman of the corporate department of the firm in the midseventies, I did not have access to the billable time of either the associates or the partners except those who had a very low or very high number of hours in a given month. The range was wide, and it was rare for anyone to fall outside of it.

In due course, every major firm began to keep track of the billable hours of individual attorneys and to use this information as a primary management tool. As profitability grew and firms became dependent on more billable time to increase their profitability, the level of expected billable hours grew.

Today the practice of law for major business practice firm lawyers has become more than a full-time occupation. Most lawyers work routinely nine to ten hours a day, five days a week, and the equivalent of another day at night or on the weekends. Most Atlanta firms expect at least 1,900 or more billable hours a year from partners and associates alike, as well as additional hours devoted to client development and administrative matters, which can easily add up to between 2,400 and 2,600 hours a year committed to the practice of law. The largest firms officially give four weeks of vacation a year, but many lawyers do not take advantage of it. A 1,900 billable hour year averages 39.6 billable hours a week, 48 weeks a year. Continuing legal education, personal practice management, client development, and other administrative work can easily add another 15 hours a week to the total. A number of firms in New York (and elsewhere) admit to requiring 2,000 billable hours a year, and some expect more.[1] Occasionally one finds especially compulsive lawyers who bill in excess of 3,000 hours a year. A prominent partner in a major Chicago firm was recently reported to have billed an unbelievable 6,022 hours in 1993.[2] Twenty-five hundred billable hours a year is fifty billable hours a week, fifty weeks a year. Three thousand billable hours a year is sixty billable hours a week, fifty weeks a year. Six thousand billable hours a year is 120 billable hours a week or 17+ hours a day, seven days a week, 50 weeks a year.

From the lawyer's point of view, even at 1,600 billable hours a year, many other worthy things are crowded out of one's life. It cannot be in the long-term best interest of the individual lawyer to work hard and long enough to generate 1,900 plus billable hours a year, year after year. In fact, many lawyers working this hard have little time for their families, their communities, or themselves. At some point, the sacrifices required to stay on top and to earn top dollars are not compensable. When you have no time for yourself or for relationships with others, there is no monetary compensation that can adequately take the place of what is missing from your life. But people who have made such sacrifices have few ways to keep score other than the money they earn, and as the only available reward for their sacrifice, they expect even higher compensation.

The expectation of 1,900 billable hours a year – much less the higher numbers expected by many firms – year in and year out is unsustainable. Few if any individuals can stand this sort of pressure throughout a forty-year career. If firms require their lawyers to consistently bill 1,900 hours a year and do all of the other things they have to do, the lawyers will develop emotional and physical disabilities, and they and their clients also run the risk of padded time and overworked cases. In any event, efficiency declines as hours increase beyond a reasonable point, and in the process clients pay more for less.

Stories of lawyer burnout have become commonplace. Polls by bar associations and anecdotal evidence suggest widespread dissatisfaction by lawyers with the practice of law. A survey of New Jersey lawyers in 1990 showed that 23 percent planned to leave the practice before they retire; a poll in Maryland in 1988 showed that almost one-third of the lawyers surveyed were not sure they wanted to continue to practice; and in North Carolina in 1990 a survey revealed that 23 percent of those responding said they would not choose to be a lawyer again if they could start over.[3]

In 1991, the Younger Lawyer Division of the American Bar

Association published a report entitled "At the Breaking Point." The report concludes that hours are too long, but it holds out the potential for reducing hours while maintaining current levels of compensation by "working smarter," "value billing," and compensation techniques that encourage efficiency. They want to have their cake and eat it, too. It is not possible for a significant percentage of the business practice lawyers in the country to achieve such objectives.

It is fashionable for associates and many partners to be disgruntled with the practice of law. When asked to articulate the basis for such feelings, young lawyers are often not certain about their complaints. The amount of time they are required to spend at their jobs is the primary one. Yet there are other young people with equally demanding jobs and substantially less pay who seem happier than many young lawyers.

Many big-firm lawyers and their families raise their standard of living to match their income, and then, if their income declines, they are unable to make the adjustment down to a lower level of compensation, even though it may be a glorious income by most American standards. Although lawyers cannot expect sympathy, such problems are real to the lawyers, and many deal with them poorly.

Many partners in major practice firms reject as unrealistic the thought that working hours can or should be reduced. They describe the practice of law as time-intensive and believe that today's working conditions cannot and should not be changed. This attitude, so prevalent in many sectors of the profession, clearly ignores evidence that on the whole working conditions are unsatisfactory, that they have not always been as they are now, and that most lawyers in the past did not bill as many hours as they are expected to bill today.

Many lawyers would say that long hours are a result of client demands. Sometimes they cannot be avoided. But the constant long hours that are now the norm are a result of decisions made by the firms about staffing, compensation, and how work is to be performed. These decisions could, of course, be adjusted if firms wished to do so. Working conditions are the product of the economic expectations of the lawyers controlling the firms. By choosing the path of very high compensation, lawyers are choosing very long hours as well.

I think it unlikely that further increases in associate leverage and billable time will be a viable strategy for maintaining or increasing profitability for partners. Clearly, clients would be better served if their law firms required fewer billable hours of their lawyers and used less leverage. There is little doubt that the pressure to record high billable hours reduces the value received by clients for their money. More time is billed for less value by padding (whether intended or not), by overworking files (grazing), or by tired legal minds struggling to turn out one more memo long after they should have called it a day.

Does anyone really believe that a mind can be as sharp and insightful ten-hour day after ten-hour day as it can be during the first eight hours? On occasion this can be achieved as people rise to the challenge of a difficult and interesting problem, but the rush of adrenalin ebbs when such hours become routine. The increase in billable hour requirements has been a significant factor in reducing the ratio of value to cost in the relationship between private practice lawyers and their clients. Clients have been paying a lot of money for tired lawyers, and many are hiring their own lawyers in-house in the expectation of getting more value for their money.

TEMPORARY CLIENTS, TEMPORARY PARTNERS

Major firms are much less stable than they were thirty years ago. Many longtime clients have moved some or all of their business to other firms. Most of the larger clients, and many of the smaller ones, have hired lawyers in-house and are, with certain notable exceptions, continuing to take their legal business in-house. As a result, fewer "firm clients" give their allegiance to law firms as institutions.

Because of increasing specialization, the work a particular lawyer does for a particular client may be only a part of that client's business and may be the only work done for that client at the firm. This makes it easier for the partner controlling work to move the business than it would have been in an era when many firm lawyers were involved in representing a particular client in many different areas of the client's work. Firm "rainmakers" (lawyers who bring in clients) are demanding a higher percentage of the profits from the business they control. Lawyers within a firm who control the business of a particular client can move to another firm and take that valuable business with them. Partners without their own clients find it hard in many firms to maintain their position and compensation.

Many young lawyers have been attracted to the profession by the extraordinary compensation paid at all levels in major business practice firms. They believe they are entitled to the level of profits now being generated by their firms and to even more, and they are reshaping their firms so that they can realize their expectations. Because it has not been possible to maintain or increase profits by further increases in associate leverage, law firms are now being pressured by younger partners and by some of the more successful older partners to reduce the number of partners. We have already seen new standards and expectations for partners and the ousting of many partners under circumstances that were unthinkable even ten years ago. Senior partners who have produced for their firms for thirty years or more and who remain very active by historic standards are being pushed out the door in large numbers.

MULTIPLE CLIENTS AND PROJECTS

Any observer who has spent much time around a major business practice law firm knows just how busy everyone is (dare I say frazzled?), how many projects everyone is working on, and how many administrative demands must be met. It is not just a matter of long hours. It is also a matter of how many things you can keep in your mind at one time and manage in a competent way. Extraordinarily disciplined and intelligent people may thrive in such an environment for a while, but it is difficult for anyone to sustain such commitment and discipline over a forty-year career.

With few exceptions every lawyer, whether working inside for a company or outside for a firm, is expected to manage several projects simultaneously. Shifting from one project to another and back again or working on five or ten different matters a day is more difficult than working on one big project at a time. The most important legal work requires intense concentration. To be interrupted by an entirely different matter involving different people, facts, and principles of law challenges even lawyers with the greatest intellectual capacity and discipline. Keeping an accurate record of the time spent on each project under these circumstances only increases the stress.

Persons unfamiliar with the intense competitive pressures in the profession today might suggest that the lawyer identify his most important project and focus on it, leaving his other projects until another day. Although one of a lawyer's projects may seem more significant than the others, clients do not know what else the lawyer is working on and, at least for the clients of the private practice lawyer, they cannot be told without breaking the confidence of other clients. Even if they know what else their lawyer has to accomplish, why should clients accept subordinate status for their project when every other major firm in town, and many from other cities, have made known their desire to do the client's work, often with extravagant promises of priority service? Given the episodic nature of the firms' relationships with many of their clients, the inadequate supply of work to keep all of the major firms busy at the level of activity to which they have become accustomed, and the intense competition for the work that exists, few lawyers are willing to take the chance of losing any good client. Consequently, every project has a high priority.

HIGH PERFORMANCE REQUIREMENTS

Lawyers are asked to handle many projects because their clients (be they executives or in-house lawyers) cannot or do not want to take the project on themselves. These projects often require much attention to detail; mastering and working with complex statutes and regulations written in lengthy, turgid prose; and reviewing hundreds or thousands of pages of documents in search of a critical error or fact, often under intense time pressures.

A mistake in any of these processes can be costly to the client and, in these days of burgeoning malpractice suits against law firms, costly to the firm and the individual lawyer as well. Even many high-ranking graduates of prominent law schools do not have the intellect, memory, concentration, and tenacity to handle such complex tasks well. Those who do have the capacity feel the pressure as much as those who do not, because they are hyper-aware of their potential for missing something or making errors.

A growing number of lawyers in their fifties and early sixties are retiring early, going in-house, or finding other employment, in some cases because of a growing concern about the risk of personal liability for claims against law firms. Many senior partners are taking their accumulated profits and leaving before they are called upon to give some of it back because of a mistake made by a partner or associate they would not have recognized on the elevator.

In an effort to limit the personal liability of individual partners for the malpractice of other lawyers in the firm, there is a widespread movement to convert law firms from partnerships, in which all of the personal assets of every partner are available to creditors of the firm, to professional corporations, limited liability companies, or limited liability partnerships, in which the personal assets of the partners are not at risk for the malpractice of another lawyer in the firm. All assets of such firms are at risk, as are the assets of the lawyers significantly involved in the commission of malpractice, but the personal assets of the other lawyers are not.

IMMEDIATE RESPONSE EXPECTATIONS

Improved telecommunications capability has increased the pressure on business practice lawyers. Many clients expect immediate responses to their inquiries and to drafts of documents. The fax machine has added a dimension of intense and unbroken pressure by presenting lawyers with documents for immediate review and return to sender. There is no place to hide.

BIG DOLLAR TRANSACTIONS

Many clients come to major business practice law firms for assistance because the stakes are sufficiently high to justify the high cost often associated with their use. These clients, often doing the deal of their lifetime, expect their lawyers to attach as much importance to the transaction as they do. It is not uncommon for the lawyers working on such a project to work through the night drafting, negotiating, or preparing for trial. The pressures from these extremely adverse working conditions are intensified by the large amounts of money that often ride on the outcome of the lawyers' work.

LAWYER BURNOUT

Given the pressures brought to bear on major business practice firm lawyers, it should not come as a surprise that there is a high level of dissatisfaction and burnout. Many people assume that the high level of compensation makes up for the stress, but often these lawyers do not feel that the toll on their health and personal lives is offset by the money they earn. The continuing short supply of competent young lawyers able to do the work that large business practice firms have to do increases the pressure on those lawyers on the job.

WHY ARE WORKING CONDITIONS SO UNSATISFACTORY?

Why do so many business practice lawyers subject themselves to such difficult working conditions? The love of money and the use of income as a yardstick for personal worth have a lot to do with it, but there is more. Many lawyers think this is the only way for the system to work. Lawyers are as capable of following the herd as anyone else. There is also the expectation of the appropriate lifestyle for a partner, which is a romantic holdover from the days of gentlemen lawyers of independent means. Many lawyers without family resources buy into that lifestyle by working very hard. Another factor that pushes these lawyers is the growth of compensation for executive officers of large companies, investment bankers, and business consultants whose compensation was previously more on a par with that of senior partners in major law firms. Although partner income has increased significantly in real dollars, many lawyers feel they have nevertheless fallen behind the increases in compensation and lifestyle achieved by many former peers, and so they push harder to catch up.

There is also something in the system that smacks of fraternity hazing. Having suffered unreasonably long hours themselves, partners doubt the dedication of younger men and women who do not want to suffer the same burdens and make the same sacrifices, even if the young lawyers are willing to take less money in return for a lighter workload. The senior lawyers assume that younger lawyers committed to 1,500 hours would not answer the fire bell and work at night or on weekends if necessary to get the job done. Although I think this attitude confuses compulsiveness with dedication, these misgivings are felt by many partners and must be reckoned with.

WORKING IN-HOUSE

The pressures on in-house lawyers are generally believed to be less than those on private practice lawyers. They generally do not spend time on marketing and spend less time on administrative matters. As a result they can spend more of their working day on legal work for their client-employer, which often leads to a shorter working day. Many in-house lawyers prefer better working conditions in-house to the greater pay generally available at outside law firms.

Nonetheless, great pressures can exist in-house. Ambitious business executives anxious to advance their careers need prompt responses from their lawyers to solve their problems and develop new programs. In-house lawyers also suffer from the stress of working for more than one executive and of dealing at the same time with multiple projects. There is little pleasure or satisfaction in having to tell your ambitious boss that his favorite scheme is against the law. It is even less fun when he has the power to terminate your only source of income. The major business practice firms have many clients and therefore multiple sources of income. When a law firm loses a client — even an important one — it is not as catastrophic to the individual lawyer as losing his or her job.

Some lawyers who move in-house find that the pressures and uncertainties can be as great or greater than in their former firms. Large corporations are more prone to closing offices and moving personnel around. In-house lawyers are not immune to this sort of reorganization. A former partner of mine took an in-house job with the very highly regarded legal department of one of the largest national corporations in order to avoid some of the pressures in the private practice. To her considerable surprise, three months after she took the job, the company announced it was closing its Atlanta legal office and offered her the same job in a city several states away. Because she had a husband with a good job in Atlanta, moving was not what she had in mind when she took the job. She is now working for a smaller firm in Atlanta.

The legal departments of some national corporations are as caught up in the compulsive practice of law as any New York law firm. In such legal departments, if you are not at your desk at seven in the evening when the general counsel calls, you may be no better off than you would have been in the private practice firm when you got such a call from a senior lawyer in the firm.

Or you may be a one-lawyer legal department for a company with an unreasonable boss who thinks you should be able to do everything yourself when he wants it done. And he may not be very nice about it to boot. Consequently, in-house work is not the answer to every lawyer's dreams. As one would expect, circumstances and personalities vary from place to place.

An interesting new development in the practice of law is the movement of some lawyers back and forth between in-house and private sector jobs several times during a career, which is a further indication of the growing parity of the in-house and outside firm experiences.

6 Where Did All of That Billable Time Come From?

How have so many major business practice firms managed to add so many lawyers and work so many of them so long and hard in light of the growth in the number of in-house lawyers and legal assistants? How could there be enough work to permit this growing number of private practice lawyers (including, in particular, a growing number and percentage of associates) to record so much more billable time? How could the nature of the work performed change so that there would be so much more work suitable for young and inexperienced lawyers than there was thirty-five years ago?

These changes could only occur if law firms (1) generated enough real work to keep all the new lawyers busy for more hours a day than their predecessors, including relatively more growth in the amount of work suitable for associates, (2) changed the concept of billable time, (3) changed the way work was performed to consume more billable hours (particularly at the associate level), or (4) combinations of the above. What has happened?

NEW LEGISLATION AND REGULATION

The aggregate amount of legal services provided to clients has increased since the 1960s, in part because there has been more real work to be done. Every new state or federal law, every local ordinance, and every amendment to existing laws and ordinances has imposed an additional burden on businesses and individuals. Interpreting, complying with, resisting, and using new laws created additional demands for lawyers' services. As long as Congress, state legislatures, and local governments act as though all problems can be solved by passing additional laws and creating new rights, lawyers will be in increasing demand.

Laws governing employee benefits, employee health and safety, discrimination based on age, sex, race, or disability, and environmental pollution are among the new laws that have greatly increased the demand for legal services, and these represent only a small percentage of the legislation passed by Congress during the past thirty-five years. Most state legislatures have passed similar laws; many local governments have, too.

Some of these new laws have created new areas of legal specialization and new areas of practice for both inside and outside lawyers. No new laws have imposed a greater legal burden on business than the environmental laws. A knowledgeable observer has estimated that environmental law compliance and liability avoidance have increased the legal costs of acquiring a manufacturing company by at least 20 percent.

THE GROWING COMPLEXITY OF
INTERNATIONAL BUSINESS

Another factor affecting legal costs has been the increasing complexity of the domestic and world economies. Businesses operating in foreign lands, each with its own language and laws, incur higher legal costs. Just knowing the law of a new jurisdiction of operation is not enough. Foreign laws often impose requirements that are different from those in the United States. It is sometimes difficult or impossible to comply with all of the conflicting requirements. In the United States and in many foreign jurisdictions, the burden of resolving these differences often falls to the lawyers. More law and more complexity have added greatly to the demand for legal services.

INCREASED LEGAL RISKS OF BUSINESS

The management of legal issues and risks has become a pervasive concern for business in the United States and increasingly elsewhere. Thirty-five years ago, most businesses did not need to consult a lawyer every day. It is rare today for any substantial business not to need daily legal advice and planning. This pervasiveness results not only from increased economic complexity and new laws but also from the pattern of much larger judgments collected by plaintiffs and from a change in business orientation. Businesses have realized that resolving legal problems after the fact through litigation is very debilitating and expensive; it is better to avoid the development of situations that require a solution through litigation. Consequently, planning ahead to avoid legal problems has become an important part of doing business today.

Lawyers have become a part of this planning process and not just after-the-fact problem solvers. Many companies have felt that outside lawyers could not develop the working knowledge of their businesses necessary to participate constructively in this planning process or, at least, that it would be very expensive for them to do so. This has been another reason to have lawyers in-house. Having input from in-house lawyers as part of strategic business planning is seen by many companies as cost-effective preventive medicine. As more businesses have seen the benefits of this course, the in-house revolution has grown.

INCREASED LITIGATION

Most of us are aware that the volume of litigation has grown significantly. More and more businesses sue one another when relationships do not develop to their liking, and lawyers have been encouraged by their clients to look for loopholes or omissions in documents to find a courtroom solution to what in the past was often viewed as a business problem rather than a legal one.

Americans generally have become more prone to rely on legal solutions to personal and business problems. When something we do not like occurs, the almost automatic reaction is that "there ought to be a law against it." Our legislators have led us to believe that problems are solved by doing what they do best: passing laws. We have passed more and more laws in an effort to solve our problems, and if things do not go to our liking, we pass another law or resort to litigation. Then we complain that we have too many lawyers, that we are too reliant on them, and that there is too much litigation.

As a result, there are major efforts today to reduce litigation through alternative dispute resolution (ADR) techniques. Mediation and arbitration are two examples. Another is to hire a former judge or a lawyer to preside over a private trial of the matter at issue. Private trials can be held sooner and can be closed to the public, the decisions are not published for all to see, they can be less expensive, and they are not appealable. Nonetheless, lawyers are heavily involved in ADR procedures, and these alternatives have not significantly reduced the demand for legal services.

OVERBILLING

Unfortunately, not all increases in billable hours charged to clients can be traced to legitimate increases in the demand for legal services. Many lawyers are undoubtedly more aggressive than they used to be in charging their time at the office to one client or another. This growing aggressiveness has occasionally led to the falsification of time records and to criminal fraud. One particularly alarming example of fraud involved a ring of two dozen or more lawyers conspiring to overbill insurance companies, reaping an estimated $50 to $200 million in illegal income.[1] Such practices are subject to civil remedies and criminal prosecution.

Most overbilling is not criminal. Much of it is the result of the pressures the system creates to increase recorded billable time and the result of bad habits developed by some of the profession in charging for disbursements. In one egregious example, an attorney billed his client over $66,000 for time on the LEXIS legal research service that actually cost only $395. The client prevailed in a civil suit against that attorney, but hundreds of more subtle abuses occur each day that are not noticed by clients. The American Bar Association has become so concerned about billing practices that it issued Formal Opinion 93-379 in December 1993 dealing with "Billing for Professional Fees, Disbursements, and Other Expenses," which identified certain practices as professionally unethical. A recent survey nonetheless indicates that a very high percentage of the attorneys responding believe that some attorneys "pad" or overbill their hours.[2]

Generally, attitudes about recording time have shifted toward recording more time rather than less. Most firms have kept their time in tenths of an hour or six-minute intervals. Some firms have increased their minimum chargeable interval from six minutes to fifteen or twenty. Most big-firm lawyers are constantly mindful of the pressure to bill more time. There is a tremendous temptation to take advantage. The end result, in any event, is more recorded time — and greater expense to clients.

Where else did these increased billable hours come from? In recent times, nonlawyers have been hired by law firms to provide financial and administrative management formerly provided by lawyers. In the process, lawyer time has been freed for billable use. In addition, associate training time that might have gone unbilled in the past is more likely to be charged to the client today, and there is greater resistance today to writing off billable time that was not used to the client's best advantage and therefore perhaps should not be billed. There has also been what appears to be an inexorable trend toward the production of longer and more complicated documents.

THE IMPACT OF SO MANY LAWYERS

The much increased number of lawyers almost certainly breeds a greater need for legal services. The old story of the one lawyer in a small town starving for lack of work who becomes prosperous when another lawyer moves to town applies on a national scale as well. When there is not enough good work to go around, many lawyers take on matters of dubious merit rather than going out of business, and the reputation of the entire profession has suffered as a result.

The financial expectations of big-firm lawyers have led their firms to require many more billable hours than they did in the sixties. These pressures force lawyers to find more to do within the project at hand. This may lead to "grazing a file" – looking into peripheral issues, and reading and rereading documents without having a clear sense of purpose, or fine-tuning language for aesthetic rather than for legal reasons. It also leads to more aggressive timekeeping practices. These matters will be discussed at greater length in chapter 7.

KEEPING ASSOCIATES BUSY

It is important to keep in mind that not only has the total number of lawyers increased but the cadre of lawyers performing the work has become much younger and less experienced. We have relatively fewer experienced lawyers and more inexperienced ones. In the major private business practice firms the workforce has changed significantly with the advent of legal assistants and the increased percentage of associates. The role of the "in-house" law department has also grown. Consequently, we need to ask not only why has the total volume of work increased as it has but also why has it increased in such a way as to make it possible to employ usefully so many more young and inexperienced lawyers and legal assistants?

All of the factors listed in this chapter have increased the legal work to be done and the cost of legal services to business clients. However, I believe the most significant factor increasing the cost of legal services has been the change in the way in which legal services are performed — with a resulting utilization of a higher number and percentage of inexperienced lawyers.

7 The New Wave Practice of Law

Since 1960, major business practice firms throughout the United States have changed the ways they provide legal services to their clients, and the lawyers working for these firms have changed their styles of practice. These changes have created much of the high cost of legal services today. They have also increased the pressures on individual business practice lawyers. As a result, lawyers expect high compensation. I do not believe these changes were consciously made to increase profitability, but they have had that result.

INCREASED RELIANCE ON INEXPERIENCED LAWYERS

The average age and the average experience level of lawyers working for major business practice firms in the United States have declined since 1960. As the average level of experience in the legal profession has declined, the level of cost-effectiveness has also dropped. The average age of the lawyers practicing at the Alston firm slipped from 46 in 1960 to 40 in 1970, 36.5 in 1980. It then rose to 37.5 in 1990 and 38 in 1994. Because most lawyers begin their professional careers at about the age of 25, the average number of years of legal experience of the lawyers at the Alston firm in 1960 was 21 years; today it is 13.

Inexperienced lawyers take more time to produce a less relevant, less mature work product. Experience is a valuable commodity. The ability to relate the problem at hand to other situations, or to put a particular case in perspective, heightens the value of a lawyer's work product. Knowledge of the evolution of a statutory scheme permits a seasoned lawyer to understand the intent and purpose of a particular piece of legislation and to recognize issues that would not be obvious to a less experienced lawyer.

Most major firms assign much of their research to inexperienced associates whose research skills are presumed to be high because the reading and analyzing of cases and statutes is a large part of what one does in law school. Consequently, a new lawyer's research skills would presumably be higher than any other skill he or she may possess. From the firm's point of view it is also the best way to introduce a new associate to the practice of law. Nonetheless, it would be incorrect to assume that an inexperienced lawyer is the best researcher for every job. If the point at issue is novel or subtle, or both, it may be over the head and out of the focus of an inexperienced lawyer. I have seen many hours invested in research by inexperienced lawyers, hours that have not added any value to the resolution of the issues at hand.

I recall one difficult question under the federal securities laws that I knew was novel. I asked a younger partner at one of my former firms to think about the issue and to consider how we might approach it. Instead of thinking, he assigned it as a research project to an associate who lacked even the basic knowledge that the question had not been decided in the cases. The young lawyer spent many hours in research and produced a long memorandum that was of considerably less value than an article on the general subject available in several books in our library.

My younger partner, having reviewed the memo, realized that we had a considerable amount of time invested in a worthless product. He then called in a senior associate and asked him to rewrite the memo. After considerably more time, the experienced associate converted the memorandum into a useful general treatise on the law in question, approximately on a par with one of the better texts (upon which he no doubt relied) but which still did not shed any light on how to resolve the issue at hand. Only then did the younger partner attempt to think about the unique problem with which we were faced. Most of the time invested to that point had been wasted.

I remember another instance at one of my former firms where a client had an issue under the interstate garnishment law passed by the federal government to assist in the collection of child support payments. I knew nothing about the statute and turned the project over to a senior associate who worked with me on the client's affairs. He knew nothing about it either, and after having reviewed the file, he took it to another senior associate who had experience in state garnishment proceedings but not with this particular procedure. She also reviewed the file and decided she could not contribute to an answer, and she turned the file over to a junior associate who also knew nothing about it.

The third associate reviewed the file and attempted to obtain a practical answer by calling some of the parties involved. He did not obtain any useful information in that process. Then he assigned the job of finding the statute and analyzing it to a summer clerk who spent approximately twenty hours working on the project. His work then filtered back up through the other associates to the original senior associate, who used the work to prepare a memo advising the client. The end result was correct advice to the client that involved the possible withholding of less than $100 from the paycheck of an employee of the client and a proposed bill, based on the standard hourly rates of the firm, of well over $1,000.

I was concerned when I saw the size of the proposed bill compared with the value of the advice to the client. There was great resistance to reducing the bill because, after all, the work had been done. In order to have a basis for evaluating the appropriateness of the bill, I decided to research it myself. I went to the federal code and found the statute and then the relevant regulations. Within a half hour I had found out enough about the statute to know that the advice we had rendered was correct. Had I been relying wholly on my own efforts I would have spent at least another half hour on the project and I would have called the client with our advice. All of that would have cost the client between $250 and $350 for a quicker answer.

I believe this sort of situation arises far too often. These examples illustrate the inherent wastefulness in a process of trying to find the least expensive lawyer to handle the matter. There is a cost in that process. Even though I had no experience with the statute in question, when I focused on the issue I had the confidence to attack the problem directly and to reach a conclusion quickly. Nonetheless, had I done the work myself from the beginning, the cost would still have exceeded the economic value of the answer to the client. However, because the question would almost certainly arise again and again, the client might ultimately realize the value of its investment.

I recall another situation at a former firm where I needed a confidentiality agreement for a client who badly needed additional investment capital immediately. I went to one of my younger partners and asked him to arrange for the production of the agreement because I was otherwise occupied. I told him of the circumstances but did not make a sufficient point of the urgency of the investment to our client. My partner called in a senior associate who, without adequate instruction, went off to create the perfect confidentiality agreement. He studied several agreements and selected points from each that he thought would protect our client's interests.

The resulting agreement was long, legalistic, and complex and had consumed a lot of time in its preparation. When it was delivered to me I realized that it did not serve our client's interest because of its length and complexity. A prospective investor would have had to submit the agreement to its legal department for review, and because of its length and complexity, it was unlikely that it could be reviewed quickly. Consequently, I reduced the agreement by two-thirds, retaining only the critical requirements.

The purpose of this review of a few past management mistakes is not to suggest that I was a better lawyer than the others involved. I was also at fault in each case for not taking the time to explain the issue and the circumstances adequately or to give clear instructions. What I hope the examples illustrate is the inherent inefficiencies of the multitiered law firm and the difficulties of managing the work of younger, less experienced lawyers. To manage them correctly often requires more time and effort of senior attorneys than they are willing or able to give. In each case, the clients would have been better served, and probably at a lower cost, if their work had been performed by a more experienced lawyer who had taken the time to think about the project and to plan his or her efforts in advance.

As routine work and counseling have gone in-house, and as the law has become more voluminous and complex, it has become harder to find work that is suitable for young associates recently graduated from law school. Consequently, the major business practice firms have found it necessary to assign each new associate to a narrow practice area, sometimes with the associate's willing consent and sometimes without it. Very few firms make a pretense of giving their associates broad training in the law today. The earlier development of associate expertise by focusing their work in a narrow area has enabled firms to utilize younger lawyers to do a higher percentage of the legal work left to be done by outside counsel. This has been important in making leverage work for the firms.

I do not believe that the spread between the 1995 starting associate billing rate in Atlanta of $110 an hour and the top partner rate at $315 to $325 properly reflects the difference in the value of the professional skills of a starting lawyer versus one with thirty years of seasoning and experience. Assuming the partner has maintained a high level of expertise, a ratio of 4:1 or 5:1 in many cases would be more appropriate. The ratio in 1970 was 3.3:1 versus a ratio today of 2.95:1.

In part the issue is how fast a project can be accomplished by an experienced lawyer versus an inexperienced one, and in part it is a question of the quality of the execution. Today, if a senior lawyer can do a project in one-third of the time it would take a new associate, the client is better off from a cost standpoint in using the more experienced lawyer. In addition, the quality of execution is likely to be higher if done by the more experienced lawyer, and the quality of the advice is likely to be higher as well.

The increased reliance on younger lawyers has placed a burden on the partners of major business practice firms as well as their clients. Because of the increased number and percentage of younger lawyers in law firms, partners must spend larger amounts of time recruiting and training these inexperienced lawyers, reviewing their work, editing their work product, evaluating their performance, and seeking work for them to do. Much of this effort reviewing work product and directing the efforts of younger lawyers ends up on the clients' bills for legal services rendered.

Fewer of today's young lawyers are apt to become partners than was the case thirty years ago. Consequently, much of this investment in training by the firms and their clients is lost. In the process, the client has paid for a lawyer to become familiar with its business and its legal issues and then lost the benefit of that investment because of its law firm's internal management and financial policies. The client is then asked to bear the cost of educating another young lawyer in its business and its legal issues. This is an inefficient process for both clients and law firms.

Firms began relying on inexperienced lawyers in the 1960s because they had no choice. As the volume of work increased, there was more work to be done than the senior lawyers could handle. They had to hire younger lawyers just out of law school because there were too few able, experienced lawyers to do the work, and there was only a primitive mechanism available for linking those experienced lawyers who wished to relocate to the firms that needed their services. There were no legal headhunters in Atlanta in the 1960s or 1970s. The first local legal placement firm appeared on the scene in 1984. In any event, local legal etiquette strongly discouraged Atlanta firms from hiring one another's lawyers. The rare lateral hiring that occurred usually involved the movement of experienced lawyers from New York or Chicago to Atlanta.

In the 1960s, when firms were hiring top quality associates and making most of them partners, the clients retained the benefit of most of their investment in training the firms' young lawyers about their businesses and legal issues. It was also an advantage for the associates, who were more likely to get meaningful client contact early in their careers under these circumstances. The cost-effectiveness of the legal services to clients of major business practice firms decreased when the firms started hiring many more inexperienced lawyers and terminating a high percentage of them without making them partners.

OVERSTAFFING

A further factor affecting the cost of legal services has been the growth of inefficient attorney utilization, which most often takes the form of overstaffing projects. One of the most pressing needs of major business practice firms is to improve the management of the way in which their lawyers deliver legal services to their clients. All big-firm lawyers have been to meetings where there were numerous lawyers representing a client, when one or two could have done the job just as well. We have seen associates sit through meetings without making a comment, or taking a note, or changing a document. Specialists may sit through a long meeting, although their services are needed only for a brief part. More lawyers are thrown at projects than are required, and no serious effort is made to manage their activities so as to provide cost-effective service. '

A former professional colleague who left the practice to become a business executive told me the following story. He had met with a senior partner of a major firm to settle on a strategy to be employed at an important upcoming meeting. "The senior lawyer brought with him a young associate who knew nothing of the facts, and who never spoke a word nor made a single note; he didn't even have a card (which I asked for at the end of the session so I could remember his name), though he offered to have one delivered to me *by courier* (at my expense undoubtedly) immediately upon his return to his office." Not surprisingly, my friend refused the delivery of the card and refused to pay for the associate's attendance at the meeting.

Another aspect of the problem of inefficient utilization is excessive specialization. This problem results in part from the efforts of large firms to compensate for their growing reliance on inexperienced lawyers by requiring earlier and narrower specialization. The practice of assigning small pieces of larger projects to a number of lawyers can be very inefficient. It is difficult for any one of the lawyers assigned to the project to do his or her part without an understanding of all the facts of the matter. Consequently, it is necessary to have orientation and status meetings for the various participants. These meetings are hard to schedule, and they rarely start on time. Lawyers sit around with their meters running waiting for their colleagues to assemble. Of course, these lawyers should not start billing their time to the client until the meeting actually begins. Some do, and some do not. Generally, it would be better to have fewer lawyers assigned to the project and to have those assigned more heavily involved.

To the extent that clients have been willing to pay for the time of every lawyer present at meetings and for orientation and status meetings, the firms have not had any incentive to work more efficiently. I recall one meeting at the New York Palace Hotel where more than ten partners from a major New York firm spent four hours waiting for their respective opportunities to address their particular issue at what was a remarkably expensive meeting for the client.

Some clients believe that their lawyers spend excessive amounts of time sitting around discussing their projects. These clients have responded to what they view as excessive internal conferences by refusing to pay for such conferences. This is an instinctive response to one aspect of overstaffing and excessive compartmentalization and specialization. However, some such conferencing is absolutely necessary today to the efficient management of any but the simplest matter. No lawyer can possess all of the knowledge and experience necessary to handle large and complex projects. All large firms have specialists who possess the requisite knowledge and experience, and they must be drawn into the matter if it is to be handled properly and cost-effectively. Law firms may invite clients to respond adversely to bills for conferences by not adequately identifying the nature and purpose of the conferences.

The effect of refusing to pay for appropriate conferences is to push your lawyer to search out the needed information and law on his own when it could have been obtained and brought to bear at less expense and in a more useful way by an appropriate conference. It is very difficult for the client to make such judgments. The client should be dealing with a lawyer in whom it has confidence with respect to such matters. Is the lawyer representing the client's interest or his own?

EXCESSIVE RESEARCH

Large law firms do a lot of research. Much of it is necessary for the firm to advise its clients properly. There are three problems with this process: (1) firms often do a poor job of reusing their prior work, (2) clients often have difficulty using the research, and (3) the research is often excessive. Our methods of legal education contribute to the third problem.

Most law schools use the casebook method to instruct. This means that students learn the law by reading excerpts from actual judicial opinions, as opposed to reading textbooks that talk about general legal principles. In due course, textbooks are used to some extent, but students are taught that it is better to discover the law by reading the actual cases than by reading secondary sources such as textbooks, articles, and newsletters. These attitudes learned in law school carry over into practice. For a practicing lawyer faced with a particular problem to go about learning the law by reading cases alone is usually not the most cost-effective way to do it. On the other hand, for an experienced lawyer who understands the area and who knows the statutes and the preceding case law, reading the new cases (and perhaps a new law review article) is often the best thing to do.

Over the course of years, a large business practice law firm will conduct an enormous amount of research. As the size of law firms has increased, so has the amount and scope of their collective research. How does a large law firm keep track of the research it has already done and the resulting knowledge that has been generated so it is not necessary to repeat the same research the next time a similar problem arises? Clients would expect major firms to have well-established systems for managing their accumulated research so it could easily be reaccessed and reused. The problems of doing so are much more complicated than might appear on the surface, and most major firms are still seeking a good solution to the problem. Some of the large London firms have hired lawyers to work full time at cataloging, filing, and recovering the research of their firms.

In 1963, accumulating and reusing legal research was a problem that most firms did not worry about. When I returned to the Alston firm after a tour of duty in the U.S. Army, I was assigned responsibility for assisting clients in responding to summonses of garnishment. Garnishment is a legal process by which a party that has obtained a judgment against a second party can make a claim against a third party who may owe money to the second party in order to collect those monies in payment of the first party's claim. The Georgia law of garnishments had remained unchanged for more than thirty years and was relatively uncomplicated.

The firm had quite a bit of work of this sort because it represented the largest bank in the state, and garnishments were often filed against the bank accounts of persons who owed money to the defendant in the underlying case. Although the firm had been doing this work for many years, when I assumed responsibility for it I was given only one file containing a single slim memo dealing with the conflicts between the state garnishment law and the federal bankruptcy law. Although lawyers in the firm had researched many issues involving the interpretation of the state garnishment law over many years, almost none of that work had been preserved in a way that made it available to me, and I had to do it all over again at the expense of our clients who used these services. I vowed not to repeat this mistake. Over the next two years I kept copies of all my research on garnishment issues and annotated those memos to reflect my experience with the various problems faced. When the assignment was passed on to a younger associate, he received a notebook full of memos and practical advice tested in actual situations.

Ideally, every lawyer and every law firm would develop such a resource for each area of practice. This is more easily said than done, however, and the larger the firm, the more difficult the task. Very few firms have found an effective way to accumulate, catalog, and update their research resources.

In the mid-1960s the Alston firm started keeping legal-sized notebooks containing all memoranda prepared on various legal subjects as well as notebooks of forms to supplement the various form books kept in the library. These notebooks grew rapidly and soon became difficult to maintain. With the law constantly changing, some memos and forms became obsolete overnight. Without some process to identify those items that were no longer current, and to replace obsolete information with current information, the memo files could become a problem and, potentially, a liability rather than an asset. The sheer volume of the memos was a serious problem.

It is often difficult to get the lawyers who have prepared memoranda or agreements to turn them in to a file library, and it is even more difficult to get them to take the time necessary to categorize the documents for indexing purposes. It is practically impossible to get a lawyer to take the time to identify obsolete material in the files and to remove it.

One does not accumulate billable time by preparing indexes to legal memoranda and, of course, billable projects are given precedence. Consequently, some firms have employed librarians or other staff to do the job, but the skill level of people hired for this work is often lower than that of lawyers, and they often do not have any actual experience with the issues researched. As a result, the indexing and classifying may not be done in the same way that the person using the files would do it. Nonetheless, it is still better to undertake the process than to ignore it, because some indexing is better than none and can contribute to efficiency if it is usable and used. Many firms abandon the effort when they encounter these obstacles.

In an era when the possession of knowledge, experience, and clients is the key to personal success for lawyers, and with the current mobility that permits good lawyers with clients to move relatively easily from one firm to another, it is understandable that many lawyers may feel it is not to their advantage to share with their firm and their colleagues the tangible evidence of their knowledge and experience as shown by their legal memoranda and forms. Consequently, many good lawyers simply find it convenient not to participate in the firm file program.

Major national companies often have similar types of legal problems in several states. For instance, many companies have similar litigation going on simultaneously involving alleged defects in products marketed nationally and internationally. The breast implant litigation is one such example. Under such circumstances, the company would usually have a different law firm handling the case in each state. In order to coordinate the effort and to avoid wasteful duplication of effort, the company typically would assign a lawyer from its in-house staff to oversee the effort.

DuPont, one of the country's leading chemical manufacturers, has developed an innovative approach to managing product liability litigation. With 150 in-house lawyers coordinating some 400 law firms worldwide representing the company in 4,500 lawsuits, DuPont's annual legal budget had mushroomed to $160 million by the early nineties. Many of the suits were similar — there were four large families of cases within the total — and DuPont began an initiative to reduce its legal costs in what may become a paradigm for efficient automated work-product retrieval. By reducing the number of firms DuPont commonly retains to fifty and linking them via a computer network, the giant company hopes to coordinate the efforts of attorneys at firms in several countries or states working on similar cases. The network will provide the DuPont firms with "a common library of research, trial documents and strategy notes."[1] DuPont also expects to reduce redundant pretrial discovery.

MISUSE OF MODERN TECHNOLOGY

Today law firms have to purchase or rent a lot of expensive modern equipment to compete. Word processors, computer networks, high-definition printers, computerized research services, copying machines, fax machines, and voice mail systems are only some of the technological improvements that clients expect their lawyers to have.

Technology has made it possible for lawyers to do expensive and time-consuming tasks that were impossible thirty years ago. Before the advent of computerized word processing and copying machines, it simply was not possible routinely to draft long documents. It was not possible to edit and revise the drafts again and again. Today it is possible to make any change a lawyer wants where a lawyer wants it without restraints imposed by the document reproduction process. Consequently, technology has encouraged lawyers to create longer documents and to make frequent and extensive revisions.

As long-distance telephone charges have declined, telephone costs are no longer a restraint on lawyers talking at length with their clients and with the lawyers representing the other side of a transaction. More meetings are held because jet planes make it so much easier and faster for people to congregate. On the other hand, recent widespread availability of high-speed fax machines has begun to reduce the need for meetings.

To the extent computerized legal research identifies more cases with some possible relevance to the issues at hand, such technology increases the time spent by lawyers in reading and analyzing cases.

Technology, properly utilized, has the ability to reduce legal costs to clients and to increase the quality of service. Cost reductions will result from reducing the amount of lawyer time required to accomplish a legal task. This also has the effect of reducing law firm profits, but it may be possible to raise rates to reflect the improved productivity. In any event, with the use of technological tools, the number of lawyers required to accomplish a given amount of work should be reduced (thereby reducing the number of lawyers required by firms unless their business grows), but it may be possible to maintain, or in some cases increase, the compensation of those who remain. That is what increased productivity should be about.

HYPE, HUCKSTERISM, AND HYSTERIA

The increased potential for lawsuits against directors and officers of businesses has made management much more interested in the legal advice their company receives. Lawyers have been busy exploiting these concerns. Today directors are more likely to take an interest in the source of their advice and are more likely to insist on separate counsel for themselves. As a result, in serious matters, the company may end up paying for legal advice three times: once for the company's in-house lawyers, once for its outside lawyers, and once for the lawyers representing the directors. Frequently, these different lawyers cannot agree on a proper course of conduct, and the client is prevented from accomplishing an appropriate transaction while spending a lot of money to be told why it cannot do what it wants to or needs to do.

In an effort to avoid liability and to buy peace of mind in major transactions, corporate officers and directors routinely employ prominent lawyers and investment bankers at great cost, often with poor results. These lawyers and investment bankers are happy to explain the need, indeed the absolute necessity, for their services to protect directors from claims. The courts have recognized that companies and boards do not have to hire these expensive specialists to do their jobs correctly, but it is difficult for company counsel to defend such a position without appearing to be self-serving and defensive of their own turf. Most are happy enough to let a big-name firm take responsibility for the problem in order to avoid blame should the matter turn out badly.

Information about legal disasters such as *Smith v. Van Gorkom*[2] now travels by TV and through the print media, trade association letters, and speeches at conventions and trade association meetings. The *Van Gorkom* case had the effect of emphasizing form over substance — the process and procedure of decision making by boards of directors of Delaware corporations were emphasized more than the substance of the decisions made.

The impact of this case and its exploitation by corporate lawyers is an example of much of what is wrong with modern-day corporate law practice. Although the *Van Gorkom* case was only a case interpreting the Delaware law, it has been treated by corporate lawyers in every state as though it might be the law in their state, too. Admittedly, Delaware is viewed by many lawyers as a pacesetting state for corporate law issues, primarily because so many large corporations have been organized there for a long time, which has resulted in an unusual level of litigation over corporate law issues in the Delaware courts.

As a result of the *Van Gorkom* case, the Delaware General Corporation Law, the Georgia Business Corporation Code, and the corporate laws of other states have been modified to permit, with shareholder approval, corporate charter provisions that reduce the legal burden on directors when considering corporate transactions. However, most clients would never know it, because most lawyers are still advising their clients as though *Van Gorkom* remained the last word on the law in Delaware and in every other state. The result has been a substantial increase in the legal costs to clients selling their businesses. Lawyers need to have the self-confidence and maturity to advise their clients on what the law is now rather than on what it used to be and on the law in their state rather than the law in other states.

As will be addressed further in chapter 10, this situation highlights the curious schizophrenia of the corporate bar — we insist on maintaining fifty separate state corporate laws, yet we act as though a decision under any one of them applies to all. This would appear to be the worst of all possible worlds. We have the cost of maintaining all fifty systems, but are uncertain as to the impact of decisions under any one of them on all of the others.

Many prominent firms use their reputations to stampede audit committees or boards of directors into hiring them and spending a lot of money to do things that do not need to be done. And, of course, it is in the interest of lawyers and others seeking engagements to excite the fear and worry of prospective clients. A lot of unnecessary surgery gets performed by high-cost legal surgeons.

I have seen such sales efforts being made. One corporate client of mine received news that a U.S. Senate committee was going to investigate a transaction in which it had been involved. The transaction involved a decision by the board of directors to pass up an investment opportunity and to permit the company's chairman and controlling shareholder to make the investment instead. The legal doctrine of corporate opportunity was obviously involved, and my law firm had correctly advised the board concerning the issue, their responsibilities, and the sort of process they needed to follow — and they had followed our advice to the letter.

In any event, I was summoned to a meeting on a Sunday afternoon in another state to discuss the problem of the Senate investigation and how to respond to it. When I arrived, I met, in addition to the client's in-house general counsel and his assistant, lawyers from a Washington, D.C., firm that specialized in representing clients before the Senate committee in question. Arriving shortly thereafter was a former general counsel of the Securities and Exchange Commission who was then a partner in the Washington office of a prominent business practice firm based in New York City. Upon the arrival of the former general counsel and his lieutenants, the board meeting convened and the former general counsel launched into a review of the numerous types of lawsuits that would certainly be filed shortly against the company and its directors including shareholder derivative suits, 10b-5 (fraud) actions, a formal Securities and Exchange Commission investigation, et cetera.

After a few minutes, I interrupted our distinguished visitor to suggest that he had the cart before the horse, that it might be appropriate to start the deliberations of the board by inquiring if the company had done anything wrong, which in fact it had not. The legal issues involved had been carefully considered, and the company and its board had done everything that they should have done. The company had properly disclosed the transaction in its SEC filings and reports. In due course, my client had the good judgment not to employ the former general counsel to assist the company and the board of directors in warding off the many anticipated assaults.

Nothing came of any of this. The Senate committee held its hearing and moved on to something of greater interest. The SEC conducted an informal investigation, concluded that everything that should have been disclosed had been disclosed, and closed its file. It was quite irresponsible for the former general counsel to seek to stampede the board into employing him and his firm without having bothered to examine the facts. Even worse, he may have examined them and decided to incite panic anyway. He was acting out of his own self-interest seeking to develop new, lucrative business.

Unfortunately, this sort of thing happens all too often today. I have seen situations where audit committees have spent more than a million dollars in legal fees for investigations or for litigation that should never have happened. I have seen boards of directors unable to take actions they should have taken because of poor legal advice that lay in their way like a Berlin Wall.

Legal malpractice standards also have an impact on how lawyers respond. Whether or not a lawyer's actions constitute malpractice is usually determined by comparing the lawyer's actions in question with what other lawyers in the community, who practice the type of law involved in the claim, would normally have done in the same situation. Consequently, lawyers who overwork a case for their own economic advantage or out of sheer compulsiveness may raise the standard expected of all other lawyers in the same situation. Unless the courts are willing to inject some standard of economic reasonableness into the equation in our present environment, the standard will migrate upward to the disadvantage of clients and to the disadvantage of the many competent, ethical lawyers who do not "graze" their files. The law should be clarified to avoid such a progressive inflation of the standard of care and of the fees required to maintain it.

It may also be possible to change some of these burdensome situations by contract between the parties. For instance, some auditing firms are attempting to limit their financial obligations to their clients by the terms of their engagement letters. If successful, auditing firms should not have to do as much work, and the clients and their shareholders should benefit from lower fees. Outside lawyers working with knowledgeable in-house counsel should be able to limit the scope of their work and liability by means of engagement letters and legal opinions. In practical fact, this is already being done. An early 1960s engagement letter – or even one from 1980 – compared with an engagement letter today in a significant transaction would hardly be recognizable as an engagement letter. Disclaimers, limitations on scope, and other qualifications have added greatly to the length and complexity of the letter. In due course, clients may need separate law firms to advise them on the terms of such letters.

Lawyers, like doctors and accountants before them, are finding themselves the target of malpractice claims. Some of these claims have been successfully asserted in very large amounts. Lawyers, again like doctors and accountants, have responded in part by doing additional research and other work that they would not have performed in the past. This increases costs to clients. Law firms, like doctors and other professionals, have also raised their fees to cover the growing cost of malpractice insurance and legal defense costs.

The trend of recent judicial and regulatory interpretations relating to lawyers' obligations to clients is another source and cause of increased legal costs. For example, the Ninth U.S. Circuit Court of Appeals in the case of *FDIC v. O'Melveny & Meyers*[3] concluded that a firm providing securities law services to a client, in a situation where the firm did not render an opinion to the client, had a legal obligation to conduct an independent investigation of information furnished to the firm by the client. This court found such an obligation even though the law firm had no reason to doubt the accuracy or adequacy of the information supplied to it by its client for inclusion in the private placement memorandum the lawyers were assisting the client in preparing. In the absence of such an investigation, the court found that the law firm was liable to the client for misrepresentations that were included in the client's document at the client's direction.

I believe that the court reached the wrong conclusion in this case and, in so doing, increased the cost to clients of preparing offering documents. The court also placed securities lawyers in the role of legal auditors, which is inconsistent with the canons of legal ethics.[4] The case has been reversed by the Supreme Court on other grounds, leaving the proposition that lawyers are liable for the misrepresentations of their clients standing as ominous dicta.

We must hope that subsequent decisions will dismiss *O'Mel-veny's* holding regarding the responsibilities of counsel to securities issuers as an excessive and unsupported assertion; otherwise, lawyers will be forced into the unfamiliar role of auditors, and clients will be subjected to significant additional costs akin to the needless and wasteful expenses the *Van Gorkom* case seems to compel. It is very easy for a single court to render an opinion that will cause a substantial increase in legal expenses across the country. Courts should be required to take into account the financial impact of their decisions, not only on the difficult case before them but on the economy in general. When such judicial disasters occur, legislation should be adopted restoring a reasonable balance between corporate obligations and investor protection.

RELIANCE ON THE NEW YORK PRACTICE MODEL

All corporate lawyers have been influenced by the way law is practiced in New York City, in significant part because many of the world's largest and most powerful businesses have turned to New York firms for representation. New York lawyers earn the most money, dominate the setting of professional standards, and sit on many major corporate boards of directors. They are and have been the trend-setters.

Forty of the leading New York–type business practice firms (many of which are located in other cities) have been able to increase their hourly rates more than inflation, increase their associate leverage, and increase the intensity of their efforts on behalf of their clients with spectacular financial results that produced 1994 profits per partner in the range of $425,000 to $1.4 million. Nine of the ten firms with the highest profits per partner in 1994 and nineteen of the top twenty-five were headquartered in New York.

Along the way, the style of practice of these firms has tended to establish the authoritative standards for the sound and appropriate delivery of legal services. Other lawyers believe they have to follow suit in order to compete for the most challenging and profitable work and to avoid legal malpractice claims, and most have not objected that this style of practice has benefited their bank accounts as well. Each new excess seems to set a new standard of conventional wisdom that increases the amount of work and effort deemed to be appropriate.

I have attended conferences in New York where one of my colleagues and I represented our client and eight lawyers represented the client on the other side of the deal. I have attended a conference in New York where thirteen lawyers (most of whom were partners) represented one of the parties while I represented the interest of my client alone. I have seen New York counsel refuse to use any of the work product of a company's legal staff and its former outside counsel and insist on reviewing anew all the company's legal documents in their entirety and abstracting them, although that work has already been performed by competent counsel. The mystery is why clients have been willing to bear such wasteful and unnecessary expense!

New York firms have, in effect, established a national standard for the practice of law that demands that client files be overworked and that lawyers at all levels put in too many hours (billable and nonbillable combined). As a result, a significant percentage of the work product of major practice firms is created by tired minds. Most major New York firms demand that all of their lawyers bill an extraordinary number of hours. Many firms publicly admit to expecting more than 2,000 billable hours a year for associates, and many in fact expect at least 2,500: 50 billable hours a week, 50 weeks a year. No law firm can work lawyers that long on a regular basis without a decline in quality and cost-effectiveness. This is another example of more work producing less value for clients.

In a recent case, a major firm was sued over the suicide of one of its young associates whose family believed he was overworked and humiliated by "inappropriate workloads with unrealistic deadlines."[5] The court found the law firm not responsible for the young man's death, but no one was a winner in this grue-some situation.

All law firms outside New York have suffered the burden of having their clients told by someone in a position of influence that for particularly important transactions they had to use New York counsel. Because New York is the principal financial center in the United States and perhaps in the world, many (but not all) new financing ideas are developed there. The investment banking firms headquartered there naturally turn to their in-house and outside lawyers to work with these concepts. Consequently, New York lawyers often are the first to work with these new financial prod-ucts, and it is natural that they would use this advantage in pro-moting their own interests.

New York is a big place, and it has a lot of lawyers. Not all of these lawyers, and not all of the major firms, are on the cutting edge of everything new that occurs. Thirty years ago, one of my clients in Atlanta was proposing to acquire a major Canadian cor-poration represented in the United States by a leading Wall Street firm. I carefully studied the governing securities and corporate laws and went to New York with one of my senior partners, anx-ious to learn more from the experts. We met with a senior partner and a senior associate of the Wall Street firm. We discussed many issues, and I became impatient with the lack of knowledge and certainty in their responses. This became obvious to the senior partner from the Wall Street firm, who apologized for not hav-ing all of the answers and said, "You know, it is not as though we did a deal of this sort every day," a confession less likely to be made today.

Unfortunately for all of the lawyers practicing business law out-side of New York, investment banking firms, consulting firms, and national accounting firms appear to believe that New York lawyers are more knowledgeable and creative than the rest of us or, at least, that it serves their interests to curry favor with the major New York firms. A friend told me of an experience that illustrates this point all too well. He had been the president of a company seeking to develop a plan for use of its large eight-figure net operating loss carry forward (NOL). The company initially sought the assistance of a prominent New York investment banking firm, which brought in lawyers from a prominent Wall Street firm. After $500,000 in fees, the investment bank and the lawyers produced the outline of a plan that would have given the investment bank 90 percent of the benefits of using the NOL, leaving the client with all of the risk and additional fees of $1.5 to $2.0 million to consummate the plan. My friend balked at the proposal and hired an Atlanta law firm and the Atlanta office of a Big Eight accounting firm to develop an alternative plan. For less than $500,000 in fees to the Atlanta lawyers and accountants, the client got a plan that gave it over half the benefits of the NOL and, when executed, passed muster with the IRS.

The shrinking of the ranks of national accounting firms and investment banking firms through mergers and acquisitions has been bad for the country and bad for the practices of lawyers outside New York. If the U.S. Justice Department and the Federal Trade Commission cared about the adverse impact of mergers on competition, these mergers would have been stopped years ago. Most of the large national accounting and investment banking firms are now headquartered in New York. Their growing size and the concentration of their management has placed more decision-making responsibility for major matters in the home office. The senior people in these organizations are assiduously cultivated by one another and by the major business practice law firms located there. Consequently, it is not surprising that these accounting, investment banking, and legal firms tend to support one another by recommending each other to clients around America and the world rather than recommending lawyers, accountants, and investment bankers located elsewhere.

Recently I experienced this process in action. A Florida client I had represented for years was negotiating with a Wall Street investment banking firm to convert his real estate business into a real estate investment trust and to sell its shares to the public in an initial public offering. One of the issues was the manner in which various partnerships my client managed as general partner would be rolled up and whether or not the Securities and Exchange Commission's roll-up regulations would apply. I had studied the issue and correctly advised my client as to the applicability of the regulations to his situation.

The investment banker told my client that while he was sure I was a competent lawyer (though he had made no effort to establish my level of knowledge and competence), these were very complicated matters and my client really needed the advice of New York lawyers. My client, anxious not to alienate the investment banker showing an interest in his company, agreed to discuss the issue with a New York firm recommended by the investment banker (the firm turned out to be the New York office of a San Francisco–based firm). In his initial telephone interview with several lawyers in the New York firm, my client was told that I was in error in my interpretation of the law and that they would study the issue further and give my client correct advice. Several hours later they called back with their advice which, in fact, was identical to mine, but of course they did not acknowledge that fact. This is but one example of many that I have experienced in recent years.

There are first-class law firms in every major city in the United States which can handle virtually any business transaction with equal competence to that of law firms in New York. The certain difference is one of cost. Why are New York firms so expensive? Most are guilty of every sin enumerated in this book. They use the highest percentage of young and inexperienced lawyers. For various reasons they can no longer recruit the uniformly high quality of lawyer personnel they could recruit in 1960. To recruit the lawyers they get, they have to pay extraordinary salaries. The starting salary in New York for a brand-new associate working for a major firm ranges from approximately $83,000 to $87,000 a year. These young lawyers receive lower levels of supervision because there are fewer partners to supervise them. All of their lawyers are overworked and operating much of the time on the edge. These factors contribute to higher cost and relatively less value.

In addition, these firms are often less considerate in spending their clients' monies than lawyers elsewhere. When on the road, their lawyers often think it appropriate to rent a car when a cab would do at half the price or to stay at the most expensive hotel in town. A recent audit of the period 1989 – 91 by Citibank of various matters handled for the bank by Shearman & Sterling, one of the nation's best-known and most highly regarded law firms, revealed aggressive billing practices. The audit uncovered copying charges of twenty cents a page, word processing billed at $48 an hour, secretarial overtime billed at $35 an hour, facsimile transmission charges of $157,864, and aggregate charges of $47,890 for use of firm conference rooms and $29,500 for weekend utilities. Apparently the firm stopped charging for conference rooms and weekend utilities in 1991.[6]

Although it is hard to generalize, my experience suggests that major business practice firms located outside of New York that seek to render cost-effective service to their clients can provide a product of equal quality at a significantly lower price than most major New York firms.

BUSINESS DEVELOPMENT REQUIREMENTS

Another factor that has increased the burdens on major firm partners, and that affects the way they are able to practice law and how they relate to the clients they serve, is the greatly increased competition for clients. When there was plenty of business to go around and one lawyer could not solicit the business of another, little time was consumed courting existing clients and very little time was spent courting potential clients. In the 1960s client development time was often focused on civic affairs. Today capable lawyers outnumber the clients needing their services. In addition, competitive law firms are constantly seeking to lure away the clients of other firms. Consequently, all partners are expected to cultivate existing clients, to bring in new clients (thereby to maintain or increase the firm's associate leverage), and to replace those clients who fall by the wayside or move their business in-house or to other firms.

The result is that each partner has to spend much more time nurturing existing client relations and cultivating potential clients. The problem is not solely one of time but also one of distraction and competence. It is simply more distracting and more demanding to practice law and to serve the needs of your existing clients while trying to cultivate several potential clients. The pace and style of client cultivation is different from practicing law, and many lawyers have difficulty combining the two. Many are not suited by personality or temperament to cultivating clients, and they are at a distinct disadvantage in today's competitive environment. Such lawyers will end up in the unenviable position of having no clients or partnership opportunities. Many of the more technically competent are the stuff of which the "nonequity" partners and "senior staff attorneys" of the larger firms are made.

Today most large and many medium-sized businesses have an in-house general counsel who serves as the wise adviser and counselor to his company. As a result, outside counsel to such companies is relegated to the role of senior specialist in one area or another. Absent a needed area of specialization, the senior outside attorney may be out of a job.

One of the effects on outside counsel of the growth in use of in-house counsel is that instead of cultivating the senior officers of one large client, outside counsel must cultivate the in-house general counsels of several businesses and also the senior officers of several smaller businesses without in-house counsel. Such cultivation is more intense because in an age of temporary relationships, based largely on how well you handled the last job, the client could pick someone else tomorrow to do the work you did today.

Where is the time to come from for client development in an era when billable time is so important, and who is to pay for the process? Clients will not knowingly pay their lawyers or prospective lawyers to cultivate them. As a result, most of the client nurturing and cultivation work must be added on to the grueling schedule required to produce the necessary billable hours.

Furthermore, because of increased associate leverage, most partners must now generate enough business to keep at least one or more associates busy, which causes partners to spend a higher percentage of their time seeking new business, leaving less time for other things like community affairs, recreation, and families. When the associate-partner ratio was only 0.6:1 or 0.7:1, each partner had to generate far less business to keep the firm's associates usefully occupied. As a general rule, partners are expected to generate substantial new business and to maintain a high level of billable hours. Most who survive in major business practice firms will be successful in both areas.

Each of the factors discussed has increased the cost of legal services to clients of major business practice firms nationwide. However, two additional factors have also had a considerable impact on increasing the cost of legal services to clients. Changes in practice styles and strategies will be discussed in chapters 8 and 9, and the malfunctioning of the common law system and its abuse by the profession will be discussed in chapter 10.

8 Changing Practice Styles and Strategies

The way major business practice firm lawyers work has changed significantly since 1960. Thirty-five years ago in Atlanta, most corporate lawyers negotiated contracts by focusing on critical points and leaving 90 percent of the boilerplate alone. The initial draft boilerplate was essentially that: miscellaneous technical matters that did not seek to gain advantage for either side and did not overreach. The negotiations themselves were more often focused on major issues and terms rather than on haggling over terminology. Parties attempted to achieve a "meeting of the minds" in a calm and deliberate manner. Lawyers did not draft contracts that sought to anticipate every possibility in the relationship and did not seek to resolve such possibilities in advance. As a result, contracts tended to be shorter and simpler.

Litigation was managed more economically in the early sixties. "Discovery" as we know it today was virtually nonexistent in the Georgia courts, and lawyers were not able to conduct fishing expeditions or to run up discovery costs to deter the pursuit of legitimate claims or the presentation of legitimate defenses. The manner in which lawyers negotiate contracts, draft documents, and litigate has changed, resulting in greater costs to clients and greater income to lawyers.

NEGOTIATING STYLES

Unfortunately, with increasing frequency, I have participated in negotiations where the lawyer on the other side was aggressive, sometimes angry and hostile, and often overreaching. I have participated in negotiations when all of the lawyers in the room have been on their feet yelling at one another at the same time and questioning one another's tactics and character. I have on occasion found myself caught up in the passions of the moment and behaving this way myself, to my disappointment. On other occasions I have "acted" this way as the only tactic left to stop the overreaching of the other side. I have seen lawyers belittle the professional competence of another lawyer to his face and in front of his client.

All of this draws out the process of negotiation and increases the cost to the client while also draining the emotional capital of the lawyers involved. Faced with a legal Rambo as an adversary, there seems to be little one can do but respond in kind. I find a dismaying increase in the number of lawyers who are rude and offensive. Some seem to go out of their way to pick an argument. The resulting disputes slow the process and add costs to the client. They also add to the general unpleasantness of the practice of law. This style, sometimes referred to as "hardball" or "scorched earth" tactics, used to be confined largely to some New

York firms, but now it is a nationwide phenomenon. Unfortunately, this kind of misconduct has spread to the courtroom and is a recurring topic at judicial conferences and other meetings of trial professionals.

Boilerplate provisions in agreements have now become the focus of intense negotiations. Words and punctuation marks are fought over. Some lawyers seem to be more concerned with prevailing on their pet issues than in getting a proper result. Every word in a contract is fair game, and the style in which many lawyers negotiate has become increasingly hostile, aggressive, and even abusive.

The glorification of such tactics and of the people who use them in the popular legal press also has contributed to this sort of behavior. No better example exists than an article in the *American Lawyer* that quoted the following description of a successful young lawyer in Boston by an admiring client: "'She will fight to the death on every point,' explains [the client], recalling [the attorney's] role in the 1989 sale of . . . Industries, Inc., a chemical company . . . he owned. . . . During three weeks of grisly negotiations, [the attorney] tackled the buyer's counsel . . . on every issue. 'It became such a bloodbath, I had to leave the table,' says [the client]."[1]

Such publicity encourages this kind of behavior, and as a result, the process of commercial negotiation is extended; more lawyers are involved for longer periods of time at greater cost to their clients. If one lawyer in the deal behaves this way, the lawyer on the other side may feel that he or she has no alternative but to respond in the same way. Valuable time is spent berating the other side, who then uses more time to respond in kind. This leads to more nit-picking and, of course, more time to complete the project. More time represents more money to the lawyers but also, of course, higher costs to the clients. The result is a longer and more expensive process, and the economic benefit to either client is not apparent.

In sharp contrast, I have a clear recollection of a contract I negotiated with Arthur Howell, one of Atlanta's senior corporate lawyers in 1965, for the sale of a small chemical company. As counsel for the buyer, Mr. Howell produced the purchase agreement. I reviewed the agreement and then met with Howell to negotiate the contract, which we did in a couple of hours in a single afternoon. It is very unlikely that such a contract would be negotiated so expeditiously today. Why that is the case is a factor that has greatly increased the cost of legal services to clients without a corresponding increase in the value of the service received.

The new aggressive style of negotiation is often accompanied by a real or a pretended irrationality designed to convince the other side that the lawyer and his client will forgo the benefit of the deal if they do not get their way. The other side, fearing the irrational loss of the entire relationship, gives up more than it should to avoid such an undesirable result. This, of course, encourages play-acting. The side that can appear more irrational may carry the day.

A response in kind is frequently the only effective alternative. I have been in situations where I had to stage an outburst of anger in order to convince the other side that my side would make no further concessions. There are lawyers who will not stop pressing their points until the door is slammed in their faces.

I recall one situation where agreement was reached orally, but on two succeeding days "new" points were raised and new concessions were demanded by the other side. Consequently, we decided to stage an angry "hell, no" response. One of my younger colleagues received the inevitable telephone call insisting on further changes. My associate placed the call on the speaker phone and I "accidently" passed by his door and heard the beginning of the conversation. I then burst into his office and shouted that if that lawyer was on the phone asking for a single further change in the deal, to tell him the deal was off, and that we would be happy to meet them next at the courthouse. I then slammed the door. In response to my Academy Award quality performance, the other side withdrew its additional demands and signed the agreement without further change. It should not have been necessary in the first place.

A variation on this theme practiced by some lawyers is to be so unpleasant or nit-picking that the other side capitulates to avoid the pain of more negotiating. Others choose to make a major issue of an unimportant point in order ultimately to give it up for a more important concession from you. When this scenario is repeated over virtually every point, frequently with strident tone and coarse language, arriving at a satisfactory business arrangement becomes an ordeal. A "win-win" result clearly is not being sought.

Some lawyers deliberately draw out negotiations and delay addressing a critical point until late in the evening when it is anticipated that the other side will be tired and anxious to reach agreement. The expectation with this tactic is that by planning ahead and acting out their own scripts they will be the more clearheaded at the critical point and will carry the day or the night, as the case may be. For example, during a break in a negotiation involving a multimillion dollar deal, one of my colleagues picked up a paper on the table that turned out to have been inadvertently left by the other side. It was a negotiating schedule that called for haggling over trivial points until 3 A.M., at which time the other side planned to raise the critical point in the negotiations. Of course, they were rotating their negotiating personnel so that their key participants would be relatively well rested and alert when this point came. We disappointed their expectations and would have done so in any event. However, their approach to the negotiations increased the cost to their client as well as to ours.

Such cynical manipulations of the negotiation process make everyone wary. When such tactics are successful, presumably the clients benefiting from these tactics would be grateful and reward their lawyers accordingly. However, I believe many lawyers are using such tactics without pressure from their clients to do so and that many clients are or would be embarrassed by the conduct of their lawyers if they really knew what was happening. In all events, the clients could reduce their costs by discouraging this sort of activity on their behalf.

Many lawyers appear to be confused or at least uncertain concerning their professional responsibilities when negotiating agreements. Assume that, in the process of the negotiation of a contract, the other side accepts some language they obviously do not understand that does not represent the intention of either client and is favorable to your client. Does a lawyer violate his professional responsibility to his client if he brings the mistake to the attention of the other side and therefore denies his client the unexpected benefit of this mistake? It is quite clear in litigation that lawyers, as officers of the court, are obligated to point out factual or other errors known to them even if such errors favor their client. (How many actually do so is another issue.)[2] I believe a similar obligation exists outside the courtroom.[3] A contractual negotiation should be seen as an effort to document a meeting of the minds, not as an effort to trick one side into signing a paper that they did not understand and that does not represent the agreement of the parties. The failure to resolve this sort of problem at the time contracts are negotiated is a significant cause of subsequent hard feelings and, unfortunately, much litigation.

Why have practice styles changed in these ways and what has been the effect on the profession and on clients? These changes are not just the result of lawyers deciding to act differently. They are a result of greatly increased competition for clients, important changes in how principals approach transactions, and changes in the relationships that exist between lawyers and their clients. These changes are here to stay unless clients decide to change the dynamics themselves because they conclude that such a change would be in their best interests. I believe that a good lawyer can still conduct a civilized negotiation with some other lawyers and achieve a good result for his or her client, but to do so today requires more skill and determination on the part of the lawyer than in the past. It also requires a close working relationship between the lawyer and client.

Because there are more good lawyers than there are good clients, law firms maintain their size or grow by taking clients away from other law firms. Every major firm spends a part of every day thinking and planning this process. In addition, every firm loses clients for reasons beyond their control. Some clients are acquired, some go out of business, and some decide to shift more of their work in-house. Consequently, every firm loses some business every week, and if it is to keep all of its lawyers busy and to survive, it must take business away from other firms. We are seeing a growing number of firms fail because they have lost out in this competitive environment. Those that have survived and prospered have generally become more aggressive about almost everything they do.

Traditional prohibitions on soliciting other firms' clients are things of the past, although most state bar associations still have in their rules of conduct prohibitions designed to discourage such activity. However, most of these prohibitions are obsolete and could not be successfully enforced. They are routinely ignored.

Many lawyers believe that, to retain their clients, it is necessary for them to dominate negotiations to give advantage to their client. Indeed, many lawyers now see it as their job to acquire additional advantage for their clients, whether the client seeks it or not. The hallmark of this style is to press until the other side is prepared to terminate the negotiations, and then to back off half a step.

Outscoring the other side's lawyers in the course of a business negotiation has become important for the lawyers involved for reasons that transcend getting a desired result for the client. By showing up or beating down the other side in an increasingly competitive environment, a firm may favorably impress the client on the other side and in the process obtain a new client or, at least, avoid the loss of the one it has. Today lawyers take great pride in being asked to represent a client who was on the other side of a previous negotiation because the new client had been impressed with the way the lawyer handled the prior matter.

In the old days, law firms had their clients and clients had their law firms; the lawyer-client relationship was stable. Clients rarely changed law firms just because they did not like the result of a negotiation or they thought another lawyer might have been able to gain greater advantage for them in a negotiation. Lawyers as a result did not have an incentive to show off for clients and seek to gain greater advantage for them. The instability and impermanence of lawyer-client relationships today has contributed considerably to the new aggressive style of negotiation and practice.

Another development that has contributed significantly to changes in negotiating styles and practices is the evolution of the hourly rate as the basis for charges for legal services. I do not believe that many lawyers deliberately drag out negotiations in order to increase their compensation, but I think that over time negotiating styles have responded to this incentive. Economic incentives inevitably affect the way that work is done. If the lawyer is to be better compensated for being more thorough and persistent for his client, it is likely that he will become more thorough and persistent.

DRAFTING STYLES

In recent years, approaches to drafting agreements have changed. For example, in the mergers and acquisitions practice it is now customary for the firm that does the first draft of a purchase agreement to include almost every conceivable representation, warranty, covenant, agreement, and indemnity in that draft, with most of these provisions worded as favorably to the drafter's client as possible. This is often justified on the basis of using the first draft as a "checklist" of issues to be discussed. Unfortunately, such a beginning often has the effect of annoying the other side by, in effect, throwing down the gauntlet and conveying the impression of seeking to take unfair advantage. All too often the other side responds in kind, and a great deal of time is spent addressing issues that should not have been on the table in the first place. Valuable time and energy are wasted on this unnecessary effort to bring the draft to an acceptable starting point. In the process, parties who may need to work together develop a dislike for each other that diminishes the chances of their future success.

Acquisition agreements are becoming more detailed in every

respect. There are more representations and warranties, and they are increasingly more specific. At one time, legal counsel for the acquirer might have been satisfied with an agreement that contained a general representation and warranty with respect to financial statements. Now counsel for the acquirer would likely expect representations and warranties about specific components of the acquired company's assets and liabilities. Where once there might have been a general representation and warranty concerning the business of the company, there are now more likely to be representations and warranties concerning several specific aspects of the business. Where once a contract of sale would have been silent with respect to remedies in the case of a breach of the agreement, an acquisition agreement today may attempt to specify a variety of remedies in the event of various potential breaches.

Once such practices find their way into the forms, few lawyers have the self-confidence to leave them out, and in any event, doing so may provoke long arguments with the lawyers for the other parties who feel uncomfortable leaving them out. Such negotiations are time-consuming and are rarely worth the related cost to the client. It simply does not work very well to try to make refinements like this within the context of a private negotiation. If we are ever to reverse the rising tide of longer and more complex documents, I think the legal academic community must decide to address these problems and to assist the private practice professionals in solving them.

Why are lawyers insisting on more detailed representations and warranties, and do they serve a useful purpose? Most business agreements have their origins in another similar agreement that has appeared in a form book, in a filing with the Securities and Exchange Commission, or in the firm's library of documents drafted by its lawyers. It would be more expensive to attempt to draft a new document from scratch, and the younger lawyer who is likely to prepare the initial draft is unlikely to have either the knowledge or the confidence to vary from the language in such a form unless it obviously does not fit the situation at hand. The tendency is to add new ideas and not to remove ones that may be unnecessary. It is not uncommon to find the same legal issue covered more than once in an agreement but in different places and in slightly different language. It requires more thought to remove a provision than it does to add one. No one wants to make an affirmative mistake by taking out something that someone else thought was useful or necessary. Consequently, documents become longer and more complex.

These changes in style have also come about in part as a result of immeasurably greater collective experience of the lawyers in the much larger firms that exist today. If a lawyer has had difficulty with a particular contractual provision, it is natural to address that specific problem in a new agreement. Now that large business practice firms have hundreds of lawyers, all of whom have experiences to contribute to the stock of firm knowledge that can be accessed through the firm's computer network, all of this knowledge contributes to the production of much longer and more complex agreements. Recently, I represented a client in connection with the sale of a small business for approximately $2.5 million. The initial sales contract prepared by the buyer's counsel was fifty-eight pages single spaced with narrow margins and with almost forty pages of schedules and several additional documents as exhibits. Another example of growing length and complexity is the "registration rights" agreement, which at one time would have required less than a page. As a result of numerous refinements, these agreements may now be twenty pages long.

Despite occasional organized efforts to cause agreements to be worded in plain English and to shorten them, the pressures toward length and complexity seem to be irresistible. Lawyers seem to be unable to resist stringing together series of similar adjectives or verbs when one would be sufficient to convey the intended meaning.

Drafting styles are also influenced by uncertainty about how particular provisions of an agreement might be interpreted. If this uncertainty could be eliminated, there would be less need for going into so much detail in the agreements. Because of the multijurisdictional complexity of our legal system, not only may the law of the state in which the transaction takes place be uncertain, but it may also be uncertain as to which state's law applies. Therefore, much of what appears in these lengthy legal documents is a re-statement of the existing statutory and case law of the state, which would apply whether it were stated in the document or not. Un-fortunately, most lawyers feel uncomfortable relying on such statutory and case law; consequently, they spell out the terms completely in the agreement rather than relying on sources of the law external to the agreement to fill in the blanks. The resulting documents are inextricable. It is also not obvious that clients are better served by these longer and more complicated agreements. It is quite clear that these agreements are more expensive to nego-tiate, produce, and administer.

As noted earlier, technological advances have contributed to the creation of longer documents by making it possible to produce the longer text and to manipulate a much larger document quickly. In addition, Congress and the various state legislatures have cre-ated new legal issues and rights, all of which have to be addressed in connection with an acquisition. Environmental legislation, em-ployment discrimination, and expanded employee benefit protec-tions are but three examples of new statutory complexity.

Government agencies also contribute to longer and more com-plicated documents. A good example is the verbosity and repeti-tion that exist in registration statements and prospectuses filed with the Securities and Exchange Commission (SEC). Years ago, the SEC became concerned that prospectuses were too long and complex to be understood by investors. Consequently, the SEC re-quired that a summary be provided at the front of a prospectus. The summaries in turn have become longer and longer because underwriters fear prospective investors will only read the sum-mary; therefore, they try to pack all of the important information into the summary.

The SEC also requires that "risk factors" be addressed in the front of the prospectus. When the SEC started requiring a sum-mary, it became necessary to add a summary of the risk factors at the beginning of the summary. In the case of some real estate investment trusts, the SEC is now requiring that what it views as the most significant risk factors be identified on the cover page of the prospectus, although a full summary can be found on page 2 of the prospectus and the risk factors themselves are set out fully a few pages back. As a result, the so-called risk factors are addressed three times in the front of the prospectus.

Lawyers are also contributing to the "risk factors" sections' length and irrelevance. Many lawyers are adding factors that are not particularly relevant to risks associated with the issuers' businesses, and some are so generic as to be useless. I believe this is yet another example of the increasing reliance of major business practice law firms on immature and inexperienced lawyers. Lacking practical experience, which is the foundation for establishing relevance and propriety, these young lawyers add everything they can think of to avoid making a mistake.

In addition to redundant "risk factors," the SEC has also required a "management discussion and analysis" of the issuers' financial operations, which must review the operating history, results of operations, and capital position and liquidity of the issuers. Such information is already covered elsewhere in the prospectus. It is more expensive to attempt to organize this material and to eliminate the duplication (which increases legal, accounting, printing, and mailing costs) than it is to allow the document to grow in size and complexity. As a result, the documents are less useful to investors and clients and more expensive to write, print, and distribute.

How can this trend be corrected? I hope that the better lawyers and law firms will have sufficient pride in their work that they will invest time that may not be fully chargeable to their clients to improve the quality of their documents. I believe discerning clients will realize that simpler, clearer documents cost less and are less likely to result in misunderstandings and disputes. My experience tells me that business executives have a strong preference for shorter, clearer documents.

Finally, I believe the legal academic community could help by teaching students, by reference to actual legal documents, how to draft simpler and clearer documents. Law professors should become active, constructive critics of the way law is practiced and should subject the language and structure of actual agreements to close analysis. They should ask whether particular provisions of contracts and agreements serve a useful purpose and are necessary.

LITIGATION AND DISCOVERY

Litigation in Georgia in 1960 was a "demurrer practice." If a lawsuit were filed, the defendant's first step was to challenge deficiencies in the complaint by filing demurrers, or motions to dismiss. The strongest defensive tactic, if the circumstances warranted it, was a "general demurrer," which asserted that even if the plaintiff could factually document the case as stated in the complaint, the complaint failed to state a cause of action upon which the court could grant any relief to the plaintiff (in today's parlance, a motion for summary judgment). General demurrers were argued before trial courts, and the decisions of these courts were appealable actions before any factual discovery could be undertaken with the legal sanction and power of the court. Many cases were therefore decided before either side incurred the cost of depositions and interrogatories.

The Georgia General Assembly adopted the equivalent of the Federal Rules of Civil Procedure in 1966 (adopted by the federal courts in 1938 and amended subsequently), which permitted plaintiffs to conduct "fishing expeditions" with the support and sanction of the courts, to search for a cause of action in situations where one could not be made out or pleaded in the absence of discovery, if at all. In addition, the new Georgia rules permitted defendants to wear down plaintiffs, even those with meritorious claims, by exhaustive and expensive defensive discovery before the plaintiff could satisfy the courts as to the legal sufficiency of his cause of action.

The unfortunate results of the new rules caused one of Georgia's most highly regarded Supreme Court judges, Charles Longstreet Weltner, to write an article in the *Georgia State Bar Journal* advocating a return to the demurrer practice of the early sixties. In that article Judge Weltner noted: "The problem is plain enough: thousands of dollars spent in documenting the plainest of facts; other thousands spent in following paths that lead nowhere. . . . We have swapped pleading abuse for discovery abuse and are the poorer for it. Special demurrers were a nuisance. Discovery has become a corruption and a vehicle for oppression."[4]

The rules of discovery have given lawyers tools to create very expensive litigation, and increasingly lawyers are using these tools to their own advantage. A report on how difficult, aggressive, and expensive discovery can be is set forth in an article in the November 1995 *American Bar Association Journal* with respect to the recently settled litigation between ABC News and Philip Morris. In one year, Philip Morris incurred legal fees estimated at $15 to $20 million. A special master had to be hired by the parties to referee one of the depositions. Philip Morris told the court at one point that it had thirty lawyers and paralegals working day, night, and weekends to examine 2.5 million documents.[5]

The evidence is clear that the way in which many lawyers often deal with one another today, the way they negotiate, the way they create legal documents, and the approach they take to litigation and discovery have all changed significantly since 1960. It is also clear that these changes have all contributed to the greater cost of legal services.

9 Reforming the Delivery of Legal Services

Is it possible for the major business practice law firms to change the way they provide legal services to their clients to improve quality and reduce cost? I believe a good deal could be done to reduce legal service costs to business clients and to the American economy as a whole while improving the quality of service, but this is not likely to happen unless clients force the issue. Trendsetting clients must care about cost-effective legal services, and they must begin to reward those firms that deliver quality service less expensively. In response to client initiatives to reduce legal costs, some firms are responding by making a serious effort to provide more cost-effective services, but it is difficult, and most firms have not made significant progress.[1] If this process

141

begins in earnest, it should become a competitive necessity for most major business practice firms to follow suit.

The cost-effective law firm manages its delivery of legal services with cost control as a top priority. The key concept is management: a thoughtful, systematic, monitored, measured process of operation. Rather than accepting high costs as inevitable, the cost-effective firm asks, "Why are costs so high?" A well-managed firm does not overstaff its clients' work. It limits the number of lawyers at meetings, depositions, hearings, and trials to those who need to be there. The cost-effective law firm discusses with its clients the process of handling their matters and develops a feel for the client's financial interest and objectives. It tries to achieve the client's objectives by an effort proportional to the client's interest. Clients should not get $1,000 legal bills for $100 problems.

MANAGEMENT AND TECHNOLOGY

Better management of legal product creation and of legal service delivery is a necessary part of reducing costs. Management has been a foreign concept for many lawyers and law firms, but the days have passed when a major firm could ignore the need for sound management practices. A better use of technology will certainly be part of the process of providing more cost-effective legal service, but technology alone is not very useful without the thoughtful management of its application and a commitment to making it work. Law firms must plan ahead and train their personnel in the effective use of technology, which will require a temporary reduction in billable time.

The legal departments of some large American corporations are leading the effort to bring management and technology to bear on the consumption of legal services. Companies like DuPont are beginning to take advantage of management concepts and technology to manage their companywide legal affairs by pooling the experience and knowledge of their in-house staffs and their outside attorneys. Chapter 7 described DuPont's innovative initiative to reduce the costs of managing the deluge of lawsuits filed against it. What was not mentioned is that, in return for being selected as one of DuPont's principal firms, the firms have agreed to reduce their normal billing rates by 15 percent. As an incentive for the firms to become an integral part of the network and to discount their fees, DuPont will funnel nearly all of its outside legal work to them. I expect that the other major corporate clients of these firms will ask for similar discounts in due course, which will inevitably reduce the profitability of such law firms.

DuPont's approach, combining better management and technology, will permit and require its law firms to make their work product on DuPont cases available to a common library and will require that the firms make use of the work done by others, adjusted to fit the needs of their particular jurisdiction. This will eliminate situations in which law firms in multiple states are independently researching the case law of the fifty states and the federal courts in preparation for their nearly identical cases. A good firm will have already done the work, the research will be available, and DuPont's law firms will be required to use it. In the process, improvements will be made and shared. DuPont will no longer pay multiple times for the same work done by different firms.

In addition, DuPont's legal department will be better able to monitor and compare the costs, quality, and results of the work done and to eliminate from their list those firms that do not provide cost-effective service. Larger companies faced with repetitive litigation of the sort plaguing DuPont will benefit greatly from such improved management of their legal function, and similar improvements will surely occur in other areas of practice in ways we cannot now anticipate.

Technology by itself has not made law firms more efficient. New document production software has enabled lawyers to produce lengthy documents quickly by merely typing in the answers to a series of questions asked by the program. Standardized loan agreements for bank clients, for example, can now be done in this way. However, most firms and lawyers will have to improve their management skills in order to use technology to practice law more

efficiently. Properly managed technology can add value and reduce costs. With properly organized and structured checklists,
forms, research memoranda, and frequent reference sources on
line at his or her computer terminal and with access to the work
product of the entire firm, the lawyer with sufficient self-discipline
and organizational skill will be able to produce better documents
in less time and to recover and reuse prior research.

Developing a systematic approach to utilizing this wealth of
material and knowledge is more important than having it available. Without such an approach and proper resource management, it can be more of a burden than an advantage. If a law firm
has 100 or more forms of shareholder agreements on line in its
document storage system, in the absence of an organizing princi-
ple, it will require a lot of time to review each one to determine
which would serve as the best model for a new project. What other
steps can businesses take to reduce their cost of legal services
from their outside law firms?

Low Associate-Partner Ratios

Clients should discourage high associate leverage by employing
firms that assign seasoned and experienced lawyers to do their
work, not just to preside over an army of inexperienced associates.
Firms with relatively low associate-partner ratios will not have the
need to find something for an excess number of inexperienced associates to do. The clients will benefit from having their work performed by more senior and experienced lawyers and will not have
to pay as much for lawyer overlap. A client of one of my former
firms understood the process very well. In a letter to one of my
partners he said:

My experience has been almost without exception that as soon
as we become happy and satisfied with a lawyer, his work, and
his billing, he somehow "graduates," and by graduate I mean
he becomes a senior lawyer with new underlings, a junior law-

yer or an associate. About the time that happens I begin to see a change in the service and bill. Instead of paying for one lawyer, which could have been at a fairly high rate, I am now paying for at least two lawyers, one lawyer because he is a senior, the junior lawyer because he is junior and therefore uneducated. I know this because I see many intra lawyer conferences and a beginner hourly rate. So when it's all summed up, my net cost to have my work performed is increased and I may not be any happier with the result and in fact more than likely and in general I am less happy with the result.

I do understand that the law business requires expertise and I also understand that I ought to have the ability to control the lawyers I have working for me and that usually happens for a short period of time and then magically I am dealing through an interpreter with my real lawyer who is now the junior lawyer and my interpreter is now the senior lawyer who is there basically to cast oil on the troubled waters. . . . You may at this point be asking yourself, "Why did he write me this letter?" Basically, it is being done prophylactically.

As a general rule, the disparity of three to one between a senior partner's billing rate and a new associate's rate overvalues the associate time and undervalues the partner time. In effect, firms have subsidized partner rates by tying the client's ability to receive a little of the partner's undervalued services to the receipt of a large amount of overvalued associate time.

I find some evidence that associate leverage may have seen its high point. The associate-partner ratios in the seven large Atlanta-based firms, based on the *Martindale* count, has declined from 1.3 :1 to 1.2 :1 between 1990 and 1995. Many partners believe that a high ratio of associates to partners is necessary because there are not enough experienced lawyers in the firms to handle the work to be done. But that is a problem of our own making. We could always take on less work, but our idea of how much work we should take on and how many associates we should have is heavily influenced by our ideas about the amount of money we should earn.

REALISTIC BILLABLE HOUR REQUIREMENTS

Law firms cannot work their lawyers as long and hard as most of them do without a decline in the quality and cost-effectiveness of their work product. If firms require their lawyers to bill consistently 1,900 hours a year, they and their clients run the risk of padded time and overworked cases. Clients should think twice about hiring any law firm that requires or "expects" its lawyers to bill in excess of 1,800 hours a year, and they may wish to select a firm that has lower requirements.

The capacity to put in 1,800 billable hours a year or more assumes there is enough work to support such a level of activity. The requirement exerts great pressure on the lawyers in such firms to develop styles of practice and timekeeping that will consistently enable them to satisfy the requirement. In any event, efficiency declines as hours increase beyond a reasonable point, and in the process clients pay more for less.

RELEVANT ADVICE

Clients need to participate in the process of developing the legal product they are buying and should insist on relevant advice. Clients need to tell their lawyers what they want, and their lawyers have an obligation to help them understand their options and the cost of pursuing one over the other. Many clients are becoming much more experienced and sophisticated about managing the legal services they receive and how they are delivered. Like DuPont they are finding ways to increase the cost-effectiveness of the legal services they are buying.

They have also found that negotiations are too important to leave solely in the hands of lawyers. To do so today is the equivalent of inviting the fox into the proverbial henhouse. The lawyer's incentive to draw out the negotiation is too strong in many cases to be permitted free rein without client supervision. If the transaction is important, appropriate high-level corporate executives who know what the company really wants to achieve and who have the authority to make decisions should be in attendance for both sides at all times.

Clients rarely want the lengthy legal memoranda many large law firms like to produce, and they frequently find them difficult to use. Most of us are drowning in paper every day, and clients are, too. They usually want an answer instead of a memo. One of my prior firms acquired an important new client when the chief executive realized that when he called us, more often than not, he got an immediate answer to his question while on the telephone and a modest bill. When he asked his prior firm the same sort of question, he was put off for a couple of weeks before receiving a forty-page memo he did not have time to read along with a substantial bill for the work.

As the general counsel of a major Atlanta business wrote to me in response to my corporate counsel speech in 1990:

> The huge stable of associates now employed by larger firms affects not only the cost of legal work, but its usefulness. I have remarked before that large law firms today often don't exercise much judgment on the appropriate scope of a project. If any legal issue is even remotely relevant, it is dealt with — to the nth degree. Seldom does anyone say: "That's not really important. Let's not deal with it." This often translates into clients not really getting practical and usable advice. The primary motivation for this style of practice, I believe, is the need of law firms to have their associates (and perhaps even junior partners) doing *something* to generate billable hours to earn their keep.
>
> A major reason for the explosive growth of corporate legal departments is the seeming inability of large law firms to deliver the kind of advice their corporate clients want and need on most issues having legal dimensions. Very few matters call for an attempt at 100 percent legal certainty — which is really the only way large firms know how to handle something nowadays. Most matters call for practical, commonsense advice to

permit a transaction to be done with a reasonable degree of legal comfort in a cost-effective and timely way. Unfortunately, this type of counseling has largely become the province of in-house lawyers.

If a research memorandum is not going out of the firm's office, there is no need to polish its grammar and style at the client's expense. It may not even be necessary to type out the memorandum, much less to edit it. In many matters, handwritten notes in the file are sufficient support of the advice rendered over the phone.

The problem of excessive and unfocused research is not solely a problem springing from the use of inexperienced lawyers to do the work; it is also a failure of management and direction by the lawyer in charge of the representation. To the senior partner's argument that he did not have the time to give adequate instructions (one I have used myself, at least to myself), the client is entitled to say, "You have taken on too much and cannot adequately supervise the lawyers working under you." In a properly managed relationship, the additional cost to the client of the supervision by the partner in charge should be more than offset by a reduction in the unfocused and undirected work of the younger lawyers working on the project.

As already noted, the idea of assigning research to an inexperienced associate (and therefore the lawyer with the lowest hourly rate) assumes that the associate has the maturity and insight into the problem to understand all of the issues involved and that the research needs to be done. Often a firm has an expert in an area who could readily answer the question but is unavailable because of other demands on his time, or whose expertise is unknown to the lawyer responsible for the matter or to the associate doing the work. In other situations, the firm may undertake the research as a safety measure that could have been eliminated with the consent of a knowledgeable client. Many clients will tell you that they would happily pay more per hour for the time of a true expert, rather than endure the cost and time involved in a research project by an inexperienced associate. Thirty-five years ago in Atlanta the client was much more likely to be dealing with an experienced lawyer than with an inexperienced one.

In the last letter quoted, the in-house general counsel also said:

> As you might expect, I have many law firms approach me to do work [for my company]. Without exception, they sell themselves on the basis of their expertise. Well, all large firms have expertise. Never have I had a firm tell me that our work would be done by the partners, with only limited and appropriate associate involvement. Never have I had a firm tell me that they could do our work for lower cost than others, but with more quality and in half the time, because the work is being done by experienced partners rather than associates. I think a product like that would sell.

CONTROLLING THE COST OF "DUE DILIGENCE"

Excess "due diligence" is one of the important reasons for the greatly increased legal costs of buying and selling businesses. It became routine in the 1980s for lawyers for an acquirer to read and analyze all important, and many unimportant, legal agreements to which the acquired company was a party. An associate, working from a prior document request form, writes a letter to the seller requesting copies of everything in sight and much that is not. These documents are then accumulated and parceled out to young inexperienced lawyers to read, sometimes without really understanding what the document is about and what to look for. To overcome this problem, sometimes the associate is required to prepare a detailed summary of the documents for review by a more experienced lawyer.

This entire process would benefit from some thoughtful and impartial (not economically motivated) analysis. This is especially so in light of the poor record of success of acquisitions in the last fifteen years.[2] Lawyers often act as though the agreements they draft and the "due diligence" they perform are the key to the success of a proposed transaction. They are so organized and insistent about their diligence work that the client may be convinced also. At best the acquisition agreement is an insurance policy that may provide a way to undo an unwise transaction or to recover some of the loss, but it is no substitute for a thoughtful and thorough analysis by the client of the business to be acquired and the advantages of the acquisition.

Lawyers may contribute to the relatively poor success rate of acquisitions by diverting time and attention away from the basic economic and business decisions to be made by the client. The client's own lawyers, through their due diligence efforts, may be creating such a distraction from the real work at hand that the client may think that this busy work is all that is necessary to ensure the success of the undertaking. The *Van Gorkom* case is an excellent example where a judge trained in this same tradition concluded that the process was more important than the result and punished the defendant's board of directors for not following a script full of meetings and document reviews that would have been more show than substance. The national response to the *Van Gorkom* case was to amend the state corporation laws to eliminate or drastically reduce boards of directors' duty of care. Surely a better solution would have been for the courts to have reached a more realistic decision based on substance rather than on process.

Fee Arrangements

As the number and quality of lawyers have grown, many legal services that used to be specialties have become commodities that are available in roughly equal quality from a variety of sources. Under the circumstances, clients would expect law firms to compete on the basis of price. Until recently this has not occurred, in part because the largest purchasers have taken many of these services in-house and the smaller companies often lack the knowledge necessary to manage their legal services.

Some commentators think that the best way to control legal costs is to eliminate the hourly rate.[3] Unfortunately, no one has come up with an alternative that will work in the interest of both the lawyer and the client in every situation. There is no simplistic solution to controlling costs. The best way to control costs is to hire law firms committed to providing cost-effective service.

The surest way for clients to reduce their legal costs is to give their lawyers an economic incentive to reduce the aggregate cost of the service. It is important to think in terms of aggregate cost rather than hourly rates. Much of the mischief with respect to legal costs has been accomplished by focusing attention on hourly rates alone.

In Atlanta the system of determining fees based on hourly rates was instituted in the 1960s at the insistence of sophisticated national clients. Hours were something that could be counted and priced like eggs or bananas. It took lawyers awhile to figure out how to make hourly rates work in their favor, but they did. Hourly rates excused everyone from the harder task of making judgments about how the work should be performed and about the value received by the client.

How could lawyers be given a financial incentive to charge clients less in the aggregate for the work that needs to be done? The ideal solution for the lawyers and the clients would be for the lawyers' hourly return for the work performed to increase and the clients' aggregate costs to decline.

One way to accomplish these objectives is a concept used by the construction industry. An effort is made to come up with a fair estimate of the cost of the legal project at hand, perhaps based on the firm's normal hourly rates and the amount of time expected to be required. The client would agree to share any savings with the lawyers if the project came in under the estimate, and if the lawyers were successful in doing so, their hourly return would be increased. If the project came in over budget, the agreement would provide for lower hourly rates for the excess work or for no additional compensation for completing the project.

Why not just fix the fee and be done with it? First, there is little incentive to come in under the fixed fee. Second, I would not want to be represented by a law firm at the critical end of negotiations or of a trial, knowing that my lawyer thought that he was now working for nothing. I think it is human nature not to work as hard or with as much concentration under these circumstances. However, fixed fees are becoming much more common, and major law firms are bidding against one another on this basis.

For example, recently I have been involved in three bidding contests for the work of prospective clients. In one case a large international corporation sought a fixed fee proposal from several of the major business practice firms it was using on other work for assistance to its in-house staff on a major acquisition. The project was one that would have commanded a fee ranging from several hundred thousand dollars to over a million dollars in the late 1980s. The amount of information made available to the law firms about the scope of the project and the work to be done was general at best. It certainly did not compare with the plans and specifications that most building contractors rely on in preparing a bid. Nonetheless, several major firms from around the country bid on the project. It was ultimately awarded to a reputable firm that had submitted a fixed fee bid of less than $500,000.

In another matter involving much less work, several local firms were given the chance to bid based on a general description of the work required. Having made a conscientious effort to estimate the hours required by various categories of lawyers, my firm submitted a bid about 10 percent below what we thought we would invest at our established hourly rates. To our great surprise, one of our major competitors, with a well-deserved reputation for high fees, submitted a bid at approximately half our proposal. A smaller firm submitted a bid at about three-fifths of ours and for various reasons was awarded the work.

In a third matter, we submitted a bid at less than what we thought the project would cost at our normal hourly rates. The prospective client later told me that other firms had submitted bids that were half of ours.

What is going on? In the first place, many clients have concluded that they can purchase the same quality of certain legal services from any one of several firms. In effect these services have become commodities. Second, many firms have excess capacity based on the billable hour expectations that developed in the 1980s. This excess capacity may be firmwide or may be limited to particular departments. A firm in this position can easily conclude that it would be better to use the excess time to earn a financial return even though the return is less than their normal hourly rates, because in the process its lawyers are increasing their experience, knowledge, and skills by working on what may be a challenging project. In the process, the firm may develop a relationship with an important new client that may produce additional business for the firm in the future at a better rate of return. As long as excess capacity exists, and as clients experiment and gain confidence with the bidding process, I think we will see a growing number of requests for fixed fee proposals.

When such proposals are accepted by clients, law firm managers are forced to control the amount of time spent on such projects. Many law firm managers are now thinking a lot more about the management of the legal service delivery process and about how to manage better the efforts of their younger partners and associates. This requires a thorough understanding of the client's objectives for the project and of the work to be done and careful planning with the client about how best to proceed. It is important to use lawyers with relevant experience and to identify a good set of documents to use as a model. It is then necessary to instruct the participating lawyers about their parts of the assignment. The key to success is planning and thinking in advance of acting. This is hard for many lawyers today, because action has been more highly valued than planning, and it is not as clear where the costs of these "administrative" activities will fall.

The recent arrangement between the New York–based firm of LeBoeuf, Lamb, Leiby & MacRae (the nineteenth largest firm based in America, with a lawyer count of 519) and ALCOA under which LeBoeuf assumed responsibility for all of ALCOA's litigation for three years for a flat fee of several million dollars a year is an example of the new managed approach to legal service delivery.[4] The arrangement gives LeBoeuf a real incentive to hold down costs because, in effect, any unnecessary expenditures of time and effort will come out of their pockets. It is also important that this arrangement covers approximately five hundred cases rather than a single transaction and that it covers a three-year period. Consequently, the firm has both time and multiple opportunities to experiment with strategies and practices to find out what will work. The risks to law firms of entering into such agreements for single large transactions are high. Firms would be wise to seek smaller fixed-fee engagements so that they can hone their estimating skills and develop cost control practices under circumstances where a mistake will not have a big impact on their finances.

COST-EFFECTIVENESS

Clients working with a law firm over time, and especially clients working with several law firms over time, if they pay attention, can identify those firms that care about controlling costs and those that care about making as much money as possible. Few law firms have emphasized cost-effectiveness because trendsetting clients have rarely insisted on it. This attitude is changing. DuPont's reorganization of its relationship with its outside lawyers is but one example.

Cost-effectiveness does not necessarily result from lower rates or fixed fees. Cost-effectiveness should be an attitude that pervades a law firm as it provides legal services. Simply put, the firm and its lawyers must care about their clients and about providing legal services at a fair price. It has become commonplace to say about many investment bankers that they work not for their clients but for themselves. Unfortunately, the same can often be said about major law firms today. The degree to which this is true still varies a good deal from firm to firm. In most cases, very high average partner income is one measure of the extent to which a firm is committed to its partners more than to its clients.

I am surprised by the extent to which some clients of the most profitable firms appear to look with pride on their lawyers' personal incomes. They seem to believe that a high level of firm profitability reflects a high level of business acumen and skill on the part of their lawyers. They fail to recognize that in many cases they are paying an unnecessary premium, and that their excessively high legal costs are the source of their lawyers' high income.

While no law firm can sacrifice its own economic survival to the economic advantage of its clients, it is obvious that some firms are more concerned than others with delivering value to clients. The firms with the highest associate-partner ratios, the firms that terminate the highest percentage of their associates, the firms that push their lawyers to produce unreasonable amounts of billable time, the firms that send several lawyers to meetings when one would do − all are more interested in serving their own economic interests than in providing full value to their clients.

PROBLEMS PREVENTING REFORM

Companies face practical problems when seeking to reduce their legal fees, even if they have a highly competent in-house legal staff and good outside lawyers. Most lawyers working in-house today spent several years learning the system at a private firm. Many have developed their approach to the practice and their concept of appropriateness from the private firms, the very folks who are providing clients with costly legal services today. Consequently, not all in-house lawyers have experience that equips them for the task of reducing legal expense.

Second, client executives and members of the client's legal staff have often had long, seasoned relationships with outside lawyers who have assiduously cultivated their friendship. It is hard to change the relationship, because such change is likely to be unpleasant.

Most outside lawyers have not thought seriously about legal cost reduction. Most big firm partners have been so busy practicing law, supervising associates, developing business, and making money that they have had little time to think about such mundane matters, and their clients have rarely required it. Companies with major legal matters on a regularly recurring basis cannot expect legal costs to be controlled unless they themselves devote significant effort to doing so. Often their own in-house staffs have also been so busy practicing law that they have not had the time, energy, or focus to control costs inside or out or to evaluate the usefulness of the procedures and practices they too were raised to accept as necessary and appropriate.

If major clients and their principal outside lawyers were to sit down together and to discuss constructively how the client's legal costs could be reduced, I believe they would find ways to do so. Improvement in management skills and the better use of technology are a part of the answer. Using law firms that are not too reliant on young and inexperienced lawyers is another part of the answer. Staying away from law firms that overwork their lawyers is another part.

All major firms are anxious about having enough challenging work to keep all of their lawyers occupied. If clients will demand cost-effective service and use firms that provide it, I believe most major firms will learn how to provide it. Most of those who do not will not survive.

10 Reforming the Legal System

Unfortunately, reforming the way lawyers practice law and the way clients work with their lawyers are not the only changes needed; it is also necessary to reform the legal system itself. I will not undertake here to explore all such possible reforms, but I will focus on two changes that I think would improve the cost-effectiveness of our legal system. The first is within the control of the bar and the judiciary: the way lawyers and judges use our system of common law. The second change would be to replace the conflicting, overlapping, confusing, and burdensome law of the fifty states with a unified federal code of corporate and business law.

ABUSE OF OUR COMMON LAW SYSTEM

A significant factor contributing to the excessive cost of our legal system is the way in which our system of common law is used by lawyers and judges today. In most cases in the courts, the lawyers on all sides routinely research the judicial decisions of each of the fifty states and of the federal courts, seeking every possible case that may have even a slight similarity to the one at hand. The product of this extensive research is then regurgitated in memoranda and briefs that are unnecessarily long and filled with much that is irrelevant. This wasteful excess of researching and briefing results from a loss of focus by most of the legal profession, including the judiciary, on the meaning and value of precedent. Lawyers increasingly treat judicial opinions from other jurisdictions as having equal value with respect to a particular issue in their state, whether the opinions were issued by the U.S. Supreme Court, another federal court, or any state appellate court.

Thousands of judges preside over trial-level courts; there are over 12,000 state court judges with general jurisdiction and 649 federal district court judges.[1] These are the frontline judges who hear arguments, take evidence, and either instruct the jury in the law or decide the case themselves.

The decisions of these trial judges are generally subject to review and possible reversal by appellate courts or courts of appeal. The federal government and most states have two levels of appellate courts: an intermediate court of appeals and a supreme court. A dissatisfied party to a trial court decision generally has the right to appeal the decision to the intermediate court of appeal within a limited time. Certain decisions of the intermediate courts of appeal may be appealed in turn as a matter of right to the supreme court of the jurisdiction, and other decisions may be appealed by writ of certiorari under which the supreme court has the discretion to hear or reject a particular appeal.

In the common law system used in this country, the courts in a particular state are required to look to appellate court decisions in their state to determine the governing state law, and the federal courts are required to look to the federal appellate decisions to determine federal law. In any jurisdiction, the previous decisions of its appellate courts are binding precedent on the lower courts and on the appellate courts themselves. The lower courts cannot properly reach a decision on a point of law that is inconsistent with a prior decision of their appellate courts. The fundamental decisions reached by the higher courts in their prior cases are "binding precedents," and the lower court must follow such precedents at the risk of being reversed and chastised by the appellate courts for ignoring established law. The appellate courts themselves try to reach decisions that are consistent with their prior decisions unless the prior decisions have been "overruled" by properly enacted legislation, or unless the court decides for good reasons to "overrule" its prior decisions, which is done sparingly.

The individual states and the United States as a whole each have a constitution that is the ultimate law of its jurisdiction and cannot be changed by the courts (but is interpreted by them) or by the legislatures of any of those jurisdictions without following a complex procedure that ultimately requires approval by a vote of the people.

Of course, there are fifty state supreme courts issuing opinions and many lesser state appellate courts, whose opinions are "reported" and are available to the legal profession through printed or electronic publishing systems. Also available are the reports of the U.S. Supreme Court, the eleven U.S. circuit courts of appeal, the Court of Appeals for the District of Columbia, the Tax Court, the Court of International Trade, ninety-four district courts, U.S. bankruptcy courts, various special courts,[2] and a significant number of administrative law boards and commissions.[3] The opinions of these tribunals are published in hard copy and electronically.

THE PRODIGIOUS BULK OF AMERICAN LAW

The publication of legal opinions seems to be increasing exponentially. West Publishing's *Federal Reporter, Second Series (F.2d)*, the official version of the decisions of the U.S. courts of appeals, was inaugurated in 1925. At first, the volumes published federal appellate *and* trial opinions. By 1932, trial court opinions were relegated to a separate reporter, the *Federal Supplement*. Even without trial-level opinions, the *Federal Reports, Second Series* filled 100 volumes in fourteen years. Since that time the number of volumes has grown at the following rates:

F.2d		
101 – 200	1953	14 years
201 – 300	1962	9 years
301 – 400	1969	7 years
401 – 500	1975	6 years
501 – 600	1979	4 years
601 – 700	1983	4 years
701 – 800	1987	4 years
801 – 900	1990	3 years
901 – 999	1993	3 years

And the volumes themselves keep getting thicker! The Circuit Courts of Appeals alone contribute 15,000 opinions annually.[4] To that total must be added the opinions of federal trial and state appellate and supreme court opinions. As a result of the escalating annual increase in published cases, it is becoming difficult for lawyers to keep up with all of the law.

This problem has been evident for almost a century and grows more evident each year. In 1906 Roscoe Pound, subsequently dean of the Harvard Law School and one of the great legal scholars and commentators of the twentieth century, said: "The defects of form inherent in our system of case law have been the subject of discussion and controversy too often to require extended consideration. Suffice it to say that the want of certainty, confusion and incompleteness inherent in all case law, and the waste of labor entailed by the prodigious bulk to which ours has attained appeal strongly to the layman."[5] If Dean Pound thought there was a prodigious bulk of case law in 1906, he should see what we have now.

The double-edged sword of technology is exacerbating the problem. Today many opinions not published in books are available to legal researchers through computer services: LEXIS and Westlaw. For instance, the Sixth Circuit Court of Appeals published 550 opinions in print in 1993 and 1,750 in electronic form (the printed opinions are also available on-line, naturally). Although it varies from court to court, increasing numbers of courts are allowing citation of opinions that are available only through a computer service. The courts generally do not treat unpublished opinions as binding precedents (as though that mattered today), but by allowing their use in briefs, motions, and memoranda, judges are allowing a threefold increase in the body of the common law with the stroke of a pen and are thereby greatly increasing the amount of work lawyers will do on their cases, all at the client's expense.[6]

HAS THE ISSUE BEEN DECIDED?

The task of dealing with the ever-rising flood of judicial opinions has been made more difficult by the way lawyers are using these materials with the acquiescence of the judiciary. A key problem is the loss of focus in the profession on the difference between relevant "binding precedent" and all of the other legal opinions that exist in the world. Neither lawyers nor judges appear to be concerned with the question of whether or not there is a binding precedent in the jurisdiction with respect to the issue at hand.

Let us consider the hypothetical case of a lawyer representing a client in the Georgia courts in a case involving a Georgia statute. The lower courts in Georgia are required to follow the opinions of the Georgia Court of Appeals and the Georgia Supreme Court.

Finding the relevant Georgia cases, analyzing them, and applying them in the case at hand may involve plenty of work by itself.

However, almost without exception, the lawyers on both sides of the case will also research the opinions of all the other forty-nine states and the opinions of the federal courts for "authority." They will cite in their briefs any decisions they find in any state or federal report that they believe may be relevant (or at least sound like they address some aspect of the issue under consideration) and helpful to their case, even though none of these decisions constitutes binding legal precedent. After they have conducted all of this research, they want to use it, so the briefs and memoranda they prepare are often excessive in size, complexity, and expense. The enormous cost involved in researching and briefing the appellate court decisions in all fifty states and all the decisions of the federal courts is an inappropriate and unnecessary burden on our society.

A friend reminded me of a brief submitted to the Georgia Supreme Court by a highly regarded appellate lawyer in the 1960s. The brief was one page long and cited only one case — the Georgia case that was a governing precedent for the issue under consideration. The lawyer won his appeal. Such a simple and bold presentation would be unthinkable today.

If a binding precedent exists, the opinions of other jurisdictions have no relevance unless one of the lawyers is asking the court to overturn the precedent. If the issue has not been decided in the jurisdiction, the court is not required to follow the prior decisions of any other court. Under these circumstances, why should lawyers be encouraged or expected to research the opinions of all fifty state appellate courts and of the federal courts?

The reasons for conducting such research include (1) the possible benefit of another judge's view of the proper way to resolve a similar issue and (2) the creation of some degree of uniformity among the laws of the various states. The reasons for not conducting such an inquiry include (1) the high cost of the search and of reading, analyzing, and using the resulting information, (2) the delay in the proceedings as a result of the time necessary to do all of this work, and (3) the unknown quality of the opinions found and used and of the judges issuing them.

In my opinion, the limited value of the information derived from the additional effort, its inability to control the outcome, and the resulting costs and delays easily outweigh any contribution from such effort. Why then does the legal profession continue to do so much wasteful and expensive work? Would it not be better for the lawyers to use their brains and to present their best arguments rather than to rely on a scrap of a decision put forward by an unknown judge?

In my hypothetical case in the Georgia courts, an opinion of the Alabama or California courts, even if these states had adopted statutes with identical wording to the Georgia statute under consideration, is not binding precedent. Such a judicial decision from another jurisdiction has no more power to control the outcome in the Georgia case (or in any other state or federal court) than a quote from the Bible or from a recent best-seller. The Georgia court hearing the case is not "bound" to follow such an opinion and need not grant it any particular importance unless the judge hearing the case chooses to accord it such weight. Its only relevance is as a possibly thoughtful analysis of the facts and legal issues at hand. It should have no more value, and probably less, than a well-reasoned and logical statement of how the law should be interpreted, put forward by the lawyers in the case, and stated in their briefs. In such a situation, the judge is free to reach whatever conclusion he or she thinks appropriate without regard for the conclusions reached in other jurisdictions.

In the present environment, however, lawyers and judges often appear to be obsessed with quoting a case rather than stating a reasoned argument, and the more cases cited the better. All too often lawyers function as finders and regurgitators rather than as reasoners and explainers, and the courts often act the same way.

The courts appear to have lost the confidence necessary to make decisions without augmenting their rulings with a few supportive words from someone, somewhere wearing a judicial robe. The legal acumen, intellectual capacity, and wisdom of these distant

Solomons are unknown to most lawyers and judges, and we can assume based on experience that some of these judges are not the brightest. Nonetheless, their words are cited with the reverence of Holy Scripture.

With all due respect for the judiciary, many judges do not possess high intellectual and professional qualifications. There is a perception that the quality of the judiciary in general is in decline as the number of judges has increased, the number of criminal cases (particularly drug cases) has increased (which few judges enjoy), and judicial salaries have declined relative to the earnings of the private bar. Of course, there are wise and able judges whose opinions on some issues would provide a useful point of reference for other judges and for lawyers alike, but each judge produces relatively few opinions, and lawyers and judges outside the state or district in which they preside rarely know who the good ones are.

Lawyers often attempt to use whatever language from whatever cases they can find that appears to lend some support to their client's position. Entire cases are rarely cited because they normally deal with multiple points of law. Usually only a sentence or a paragraph is used — sometimes only a sentence fragment. Unless a judge reads each case cited (which adds greatly to the work to be done), as opposed to merely reading the quoted material, he or she does not even know if the quote is accurate, much less whether or not it was really relevant to the case before the court. Dicta often is cited as though it were a holding. Dicta is a statement in a case that is not essential to the conclusion reached by the court in the case and is not binding precedent. A holding is the most narrowly construed statement of the decisive law in the case and is binding precedent. Unfortunately, if the "best" case that the lawyers can find does not support the result they want, they often quote words out of context or they otherwise manipulate the language of the cited case so that it appears to support a conclusion which is in fact inconsistent with a fair reading of the case.

Consequently, judges (and their clerks) cannot rely on the briefs before them. If they are to do their jobs properly, they must read the case from which a "quote" is taken. This is a very time-consuming process, and it is clear from some judicial opinions like the *O'Melveny* decision discussed at length later in this chapter that this sort of diligent, careful analysis often does not occur. Some lawyers treat the use of case citations as a game without rules and do not exercise honest judgment in the use of these materials. Judges seem to accept slipshod or dishonest use of precedents as an inevitable part of the process. The result demeans the judicial process and the system of justice, and it increases costs.

The courts have an obligation as well as the power to tell counsel the type of precedent they want to have presented and to punish those lawyers who abuse the process. Under present circumstances with limited judicial resources, a rapidly expanding supply of potentially relevant citations, and an increasing number of lawyers who are heedless of how they cite cases, the burden on the courts is unmanageable. In order for the courts to do their work well and to control the cost of the legal process, they need to find a way to limit the scope of the precedential materials considered relevant to their work. The best way to do this is to accept only citations to cases issued in their own jurisdictions.

The Georgia Supreme Court, in the early 1960s, was not interested in the judicial opinions of courts in other jurisdictions. This was particularly true of federal court opinions. While some of this feeling was grounded in historical hard feeling and a surviving southern chauvinism, this attitude applied to the appellate court decisions of other southern states as well and had much of its basis in a sense of obligation to the binding precedents of the Georgia courts. I recall sitting in on a Georgia Supreme Court argument in the early sixties when the chief justice castigated an elderly lawyer for citing a decision of the highest appellate court of a neighboring state in support of his position. The chief justice was only interested in knowing what the Georgia appellate courts had to say on the subject. At the time I was embarrassed and impatient with what I thought was a provincial and unsophisticated approach. However, the wisdom and soundness of that approach is now obvious.

THE FAILURE OF LEGAL EDUCATION

The system of legal education in the United States has contributed to the decline of legal craftsmanship and the loss of understanding of how the legal system is supposed to work. The law is taught in law schools by the use of "casebooks," which present "the law" by quoting from cases drawn from all U.S. jurisdictions, and occasionally foreign ones, selected by the author because of the skill of the judge in illuminating the issues or because the author thought the conclusion reached was correct or at least worthy of consideration. In class, students are called upon to "state the case": to tell the facts of the case and what the court decided, and to analyze the court's reasoning. In this process, a case from one jurisdiction is as good as one from another. Every case is "binding precedent" in the classroom.

Graduates of our law schools practice law much the way they learn it, as do the lawyers who become judges. In law school not enough emphasis is placed on the judicial process in a particular jurisdiction or on the role of stare decisis ("it is decided") and binding precedent. The resulting loss to the profession of legal craftsmanship – the precise and disciplined use of relevant judicial precedent – has been a lapse in legal education that has been very expensive for the American judicial and economic systems.

DROWNING IN CASES—DROWNING THE LAW

The courts are partially responsible for this breakdown in legal craftsmanship, because they have the legal power to require that lawyers use the system properly. However, at least a part of the breakdown is attributable to the growing burden of the common law on the judges themselves, their increasing caseloads, and their resulting reliance on judicial clerks to assist them in the preparation of their decisions.

In 1960, there were 8,180 judges in the United States, 599 of whom sat on the federal bench. Judges were 2.8 percent of a total lawyer population of 286,000. The proportion of judges to lawyers has since dropped with the result that, by 1992, there were approximately 17,000 judges, or just 2 percent of the total population of attorneys, even though during the seventies the federal bench grew 205 percent and the state judiciaries increased on average 63 percent. State judges remain six times as numerous as federal judges.[7]

Although the number of judges has been falling behind the growth in the number of lawyers, the growth in the number of lawsuits has accelerated. Tort filings of all sorts – personal injury, products liability, business torts – increased on average 3 percent per capita in the early eighties.[8] This means that the number of cases is increasing 3 percent faster than the growth of the population, which is also growing significantly.

In the federal district courts, for example, the number of civil cases filed increased 9 percent in a single year (from 210,890 in 1991 to 230,509 in 1992). Federal criminal cases have increased from 33,000 in 1982 to 48,000 in 1992, rising 45 percent. The number of federal appeals increased 23 percent between 1988 and 1992, to 47,013. The most dramatic rise in filings has been in the U.S. bankruptcy courts, where cases totaled 380,000 in 1982 and almost one million by 1992, a 163 percent increase. As caseloads have increased, Congress and state assemblies have failed to increase the size of the judiciary proportionately. As a result, the burden on the courts is becoming overwhelming as the population grows and such growth accumulates over decades, but the size of the judiciary does not keep pace.

In addition, many cases today are much larger and more complex than cases thirty years ago. In the tort field, for instance, filings for simple automobile accident cases have remained relatively stable, whereas massive products liability class actions and complex environmental filings have risen dramatically, increasing the burden on the courts more than the growing number of cases would indicate.

Moreover, as noted above, the increased use of pretrial discovery, pioneered in the federal courts and adopted by the legislatures of most states, has made these complex multiparty cases even more onerous. Discovery is typically 80 percent of the cost of civil litigation. As one environmental litigator put it: "Depositions often run on interminably and can bring a business to a near standstill. Document production, costing the requestor relatively little, allows parties to roam through opponents' file cabinets. Small wonder then, extraordinary time and energy having been expended before the case ever goes to trial, that the average civil lawsuit runs on fourteen months, and many three to five years."[9]

The proliferation of litigation is in part attributable to a third trend: the creation of legal causes of action by legislators as solutions to political and societal problems.[10] The ability to create new statutory schemes for litigants to seek justice for various "wrongs" has been of tremendous value to politicians, who view such solutions as pleasing to constituents, easy, and cheap. The creation of these new rights has also been of tremendous value to lawyers and their firms. Rarely does a legislature pledge additional resources to the judiciary to help it deal with the responsibility of adjudicating a new class of claims, and when citizens exercise their newly minted rights and place additional burdens on the judicial system, lawyers are often blamed rather than the politicians who created the new rights.

YOUTHFUL LAWMAKERS

As the caseloads of judges have increased, judges have hired an increasing number of lawyers (clerks) to assist them with their work, and the judges have followed the established practice of hiring young lawyers fresh from law school for most of these jobs. At the turn of the century, each U.S. Supreme Court justice had one law clerk. Today, each justice has four. Clerks usually are hired directly upon graduation from law school and are generally

selected from among the top students in the class, though a judge
may occasionally select an applicant for other reasons such as being the qualified child of an old friend. To be selected as a U.S.
Supreme Court clerk is the highest honor that can be obtained by
a law school graduate. It can only happen after he or she first has
been selected to clerk for a federal court of appeals judge and
then has served as a clerk for at least a year.

Anthony T. Kronman, the new dean of the Yale Law School, in
his recent book, *The Lost Lawyer*, attributes much of the decline
in judicial craftsmanship to the growing caseload and the effort to
manage this increased burden through the use of clerks.

> It is clerks who are largely responsible for the increasing length
> of opinions. Opinions written by law clerks tend to be longer
> because their authors have not yet acquired the conciseness
> that comes with experience and practice. Being new to the law,
> moreover, they lack confidence in their insight and judgment,
> and therefore tend to include every conceivable argument for
> their position in any opinion they write. . . .
>
> This same timidity, Posner suggests [referring to Judge
> Richard Posner of the 7th U.S. Circuit Court of Appeals, who is
> a prolific commentator on the legal process], also accounts for
> the obsessive footnoting and heavy use of legal jargon that are
> hallmarks of contemporary opinion-writing. Too insecure to
> speak in their own voices, law clerks tend to speak through the
> words and opinions of others instead and to express themselves
> by means of conventional phrases for which they need take no
> personal responsibility.[11]

Most judicial clerks have been editors of their law school's law
review. Most law review articles are dull, ponderous, heavily foot-
noted, and too long. Much of this style of writing is also finding its
way into judicial opinions through the former law review editors.

Kronman notes that recent legal opinions heavily influenced
by unseasoned and inexperienced clerks are now appearing in
law school casebooks, where they are becoming the standard of

instruction.[12] Judge Richard Posner sees much of the problem of contemporary legal opinion writing as a result of the use of young and inexperienced clerks:

> The prolixity, the excessive use of footnotes, the jargon, the complicated multipart tests, the endless talk of balancing (which sounds, at the surface at least, so sensibly mature) — these are the habits of beginners, of smart young lawyers with great intelligence but little experience who are not yet the masters of their craft and must therefore of necessity rely on something other than their own undeveloped judgment.[13]

These same qualities of youth — the lack of experience, seasoning, maturity, confidence, judgment, and insight — so evident in the judicial clerks, who are the best and brightest of the law school graduating classes, are equally evident in their classmates who make up a growing percentage of the legal staffs of major business practice law firms. The corrupting influence of this excessive reliance on young and inexperienced lawyers by the courts is also found in the work of the large business practice firms.

Perhaps some consideration should be given by the courts to recruiting some of their clerks from the ranks of mature lawyers dropped by law firms, not because of a lack of legal skills and judgment but because of a lack of marketing skills — a quality that should not be missed in the judicial process.

BAD JUDICIAL DECISIONS = EXPENSIVE LAW

The *O'Melveny* case, mentioned in chapter 7, is a telling example of how the irresponsible citation of questionable authority has infected the judiciary and, in the process, increased the cost of legal services to clients. In 1994, the U.S. Ninth Circuit Court of Appeals reversed the lower court's grant of summary judgment in the *O'Melveny* case and ruled that legal counsel to security issuers have the legal obligation to ferret out their client's misrepresentations to them by citing three authorities that said nothing of the sort.

Both *Felts v. National Account Sys. Assoc., Inc.*[14] and *Koehler v. Pulvers*[15] were cited for this proposition. *Koehler*'s significance appears to be only that it cites *Felts*. *Felts*, in turn, misread the seminal case in the area of liability for securities offerings and related disclosure materials, *Escott v. BarChris Construction Corp.*[16] Although it is true that two lawyers were held liable in *BarChris*, they were in fact liable in their capacity as *directors* of the issuing corporation, not as legal counsel for the issuer. The *Felts* decision misconstrued this holding and reached a conclusion that was probably correct on the special facts of the case but in dicta unnecessarily expanded the liability of lawyers for their clients' activities. All three of these decisions were issued by federal district courts; consequently, none of the opinions was binding precedent on the Ninth Circuit Court of Appeals or on any other court but the one that issued the opinion in the first place. The Ninth Circuit in *O'Melveny* haphazardly perpetuated these errors. Nor is the mistake particularly subtle: the court in *BarChris* specifically rejected the contention that lawyers representing the issuer or underwriter were "experts" subject to stringent requirements of care within the meaning of the securities laws.

The third authority cited in support of the Ninth Circuit decision — a securities law treatise — applied to opinion letters issued by counsel *to third parties*. An opinion letter is just that: a letter issued by a lawyer or a law firm to a client or a third party opining what the law is with respect to a specific issue. A law firm should not issue such an opinion before performing a competent examination of the controlling laws, cases, and facts or, if it has not performed such a factual examination, it should say so in its opinion. Such a sensible requirement hardly suggests that lawyers cannot rely on the representations of their client in a situation where they are only one of several participants in the drafting of the documents and no opinion is given.[17] Somehow the *O'Melveny* court missed the basic point that the O'Melveny law firm had not given an opinion to anyone about anything involved in the case. Even if they had given an opinion, numerous federal court decisions permit lawyers to rely on the representations of their clients in rendering opinions where such reliance is clearly stated in the opinion. The reasoning of such cases has a compelling application to the situation in *O'Melveny*.

For instance, several cases were cited in the case of *Fortson v. Winstead McGuire, Sechrest & Minick*, 961 F.2d 469 (4th Cir.1992) (which may not have been published in time for the *O'Melveny* court to refer to it) that were contrary to the position taken by the *O'Melveny* court. In reliance on the cited previous cases and the statutes, the Court stated:

> Because of Winstead's failure to ensure accurate disclosure, appellants claim that the law firm should be liable under § 10(b) of the Securities Exchange Act of 1934, 15 U.S.C. § 78j(b). . . . Under § 10(b), a failure to disclose material information constitutes securities fraud only upon proof of a duty to disclose. . . . Several circuits, including this one, have concluded that the federal securities laws are not the source of such a duty. . . .
>
> Appellants further seek to locate Winstead's duty of disclosure in a Treasury Department regulation and in an American Bar Association ethics opinion. In their view, Winstead's reliance on the representations of its client without independent verification is fundamentally at odds with the guidelines set forth in the Treasury regulations and the ethical standards announced in ABA Opinion 346. Although language can be found in both the Treasury regulation and the ABA opinion to support a variety of positions, we are not convinced that Winstead's conduct is inconsistent with these standards. The ABA opinion permits an attorney to assume that the facts related to him by the client are accurate, so long as he has no knowledge that would raise suspicion. The attorney "does not have the responsibility to 'audit' the affairs of his client or to assume, without reasonable cause, that a client's statement of the facts cannot be relied upon. . . ." The Treasury regulations include

similar language: "[A] practitioner need not conduct an audit or independent verification of the asserted facts, or assume that a client's statement of the facts cannot be relied upon, unless he/she has reason to believe that any relevant facts asserted to him/her are untrue...."

In the absence of a duty grounded in law, appellants essentially ask us to create a duty of disclosure grounded in sound public policy. The policy apparently is that of having law firms monitor, upon pain of liability, the representations that their clients make to any third party. The end result would have attorneys stand as the guarantors of integrity in all commercial transactions, whether the context be one of raising capital, marketing a product, or negotiating a contract. Lawyers, in short, would function in the business world as designated watchdogs.

Like most policy arguments, however, this one has two sides. Here, Winstead had unequivocally informed potential investors that the law firm had not verified the financial data provided to it by its client. To find a duty in the face of this express disclaimer of verification would render law firms powerless to define the scope of their involvement in commercial transactions. The services that attorneys provide for an issuer of securities have varied widely, and counsel has not been presumed to warrant the veracity of every statement made in an offering memorandum....

The result of appellants' position would thus be a rigid rule charging all attorneys who involve themselves in any narrow corner of a commercial transaction with responsibility for the whole transaction. Under such a regime, "a party could be liable for unlimited information even though it would be well beyond the matter for which it was retained," *Roberts v. Peat, Marwick, Mitchell & Co.*, 857 F.2d 646, 654 (9th Cir.1988), and even though the information might fall under the protection of the attorney-client privilege. *Abell*, 858 F.2d at 1124. An omnipresent duty of disclosure would not only be unfair to law firms; it would destroy incentives for clients to be forthcoming with their attorneys and would artificially inflate the cost of involving legal counsel in commercial ventures. See *Di-Leo v. Ernst & Young*, 901 F.2d 624, 629 (7th Cir.1990).

It is hard to believe that the Ninth Circuit Court of Appeals could have missed all of the cases cited in the *Winstead McGuire* case. The ignoring of these precedents by the *O'Melveny* court is symptomatic of the overall decline in legal craftsmanship in the profession.

The *O'Melveny* case is bad enough from the point of view of the legal process, but the decision also would have had a disastrous effect on the cost of legal services to clients if it had not been overturned by the Supreme Court. (However, the Supreme Court's decision was based on another issue in the case, leaving open the possible reemergence of the *O'Melveny* rule of lawyer liability.) If the *O'Melveny* case had been permitted to stand, the result would have been a substantial increase in the amount of work lawyers would have had to perform with respect to securities offerings with a resulting increase in legal costs. However, even the additional work would not have eliminated the increased liability exposure of lawyers working on these matters, which would presumably find its way into the cost of legal malpractice insurance and further increases in the cost of the services to clients, all the while doing the damage identified by the Fourth Circuit Court of Appeals in the *Winstead McGuire* case.

CONTROLLING THE USE OF THE COMMON LAW

The obsession with citing some judge's opinion regardless of the source is made possible in part by the publishers of judicial opinions and the providers of electronic research, who are expanding the number and types of cases they report and are promoting the use of all available cases as authority through free use of their electronic services in law school and free training for law firms. If the law acknowledges the relevance of an Alaska

Supreme Court decision to the proper interpretation of a Georgia legal issue, there is not a strong case for stopping at the borders of the United States. Why not also research and brief the judicial decisions of the United Kingdom, the entire English-speaking world, or for that matter the rest of the world? In due course, the legal publishers will have all of these cases available on-line and translated into every major language. Where will we draw the line?

What is perfectly clear is that the additional cost of gaining access to all of these materials and of sorting through them would add tremendously to the cost of the legal process. It is now thought to be a real coup to cite a so-called unpublished opinion, which, of course, is published electronically or it would not be possible to cite it. As noted above, the federal bench is coming to accept in briefs and other documents citations to unpublished opinions available on databases. No such case is a binding precedent. Why, under the circumstances, are we burdening our legal system and legal process with these additional "precedents"?

There is a risk that, in using unpublished opinions as any kind of authority, we are voluntarily degrading the quality of the judicial process. Federal judges often have control over the decision to publish a particular opinion. If a judge decides that an opinion should not be published, his decision may well reflect his conviction that the particular opinion is unsuitable in some way for publication. Perhaps the opinion is not as well researched or as comprehensive as the judge would prefer, or the opinion may simply not be as well written or reasoned as opinions the judge would ordinarily certify for publication. This risk is particularly high in the current era of judicial overload. In any event, a decision not to publish suggests the writer detects a defect in the opinion that makes it unsuitable for precedential reference. The use of unpublished opinions as authority in subsequent matters thus may be contrary to the intent of the writer. It seems that some deference should be shown to the writer's judgment concerning his or her own work.

Computerized legal research has increased the speed with which a lawyer can identify cases that appear to address the subject of his or her concern, and the computer may be more thorough in what it finds. Nonetheless, once the cases have been found, the lawyer and the judge (or his clerks) are still faced with reading and analyzing them. Whatever time has been saved by computerized research has certainly been washed away by the increased number of cases published electronically and the computer's ability to identify a larger number of potentially relevant cases. Because the growth in case publication is inevitable, lawyers are better off with computer research than they would have been without it. However, computerized research may only have postponed the day when our common law system collapses of its own weight in the face of the sheer impossibility of reading, analyzing, and synthesizing all of the possibly relevant cases, especially if all published cases are deemed to be relevant.

How Can We Reform the Legal System?

Why has the decline in legal craftsmanship reflected in the *O'Melveny* case infected the judiciary, and why has the judiciary permitted it to occur? What can be done to guard against these rogue cases that wreak so much havoc on the way law is practiced and on the cost of legal services to clients? In addition, what can be done about the unbridled researching and briefing of all American judicial decisions that is imposing such a significant financial burden on clients and a suffocating burden on the courts?

I believe each of the federal and state appellate courts should adopt the position that the judicial authority from other state and federal jurisdictions has no special value in resolving an issue before them and that such cases should not be researched and briefed unless the issue at hand involves the application of the law of such jurisdiction. The courts should also make it clear that the failure of lawyers to research the judicial decisions of other jurisdictions does not constitute malpractice. Lawyers should only need to find and consider the legal decisions that are binding precedent in the relevant jurisdiction.

These precedents should be used honestly and accurately, and lawyers who disregard the proper application of precedent or who misquote or distort the meaning of precedents should be disciplined by the courts for doing so. Lawyers must be encouraged to use their brains and their analytical skills to propose proper solutions to legal issues where there is not a binding precedent in the appellate court decisions of the controlling jurisdiction. The challenge to the legal profession is to redevelop a sense of responsible craftsmanship in dealing with legal authority. I am asserting here not a rule of jurisprudence but rather what I view to be the only practical alternative if our legal system is to continue to function at a price our economy can afford.

In addition, it would be a sound investment of public funds to appoint more judges and fewer law clerks. Just as law firms and their clients would benefit from less associate leverage, the courts and the quality of their opinions would benefit from less "law clerk leverage."

A FEDERAL COMMERCIAL AND CORPORATE CODE?

The time may have come to consider creating a uniform federal system of commercial and corporate law. Lawyers persist in treating the laws of the fifty states as relevant to the interpretation of their respective state statutes, with the consequent necessity of researching the laws and cases of the fifty states in order to take a position on any matter that arises in the courts of any state. As a result, the preservation of our fifty separate state legal systems plus the federal system adds tremendous costs to the functioning of our commercial and corporate world.

A Delaware case like the *Van Gorkom* case can sweep across the country with lawyers in every state advising their clients as though their obligations under their own state law were the same as under Delaware law. If lawyers insist in acting as though we have only one legal system in this country, we might as well set one up and save ourselves a lot of wasted time and money.

I do not know of any convincing argument at this time that fifty state corporate statutes and commercial codes interpreted by fifty state courts serve any useful purpose other than protecting the turf and income of lawyers in the fifty states. I believe we would be better off if federal law governed all commercial and corporate issues in our country and if such law were interpreted only by the federal courts. As cases were decided, the United States would develop a substantial body of consistent law and precedent to guide business activity, and the amount of time and money spent in managing our corporate and commercial affairs would be substantially reduced.

11 Sick of Lawyers — Sick of the Law

Why are so many lawyers sick of the law, and why is our society sick of lawyers? In chapter 5 I addressed the working conditions that an increasing number of lawyers are finding oppressive and unsatisfactory. The long hours of work, the mounting pressures and stress, multiple clients and projects, high performance requirements, big dollar transactions — all contribute to fatigue, frustration, and burnout.

PERSONALITY AND CHARACTER

The personality traits of many "prominent" big-firm lawyers and law firms are antithetical to the characteristics we associated with such lawyers and firms three and a half decades ago. Leading members of the bar in 1960 were often (but not always) modest, restrained, thoughtful, industrious, deliberate, cautious, and public-spirited. Many were also aggressive and arrogant, and some were impetuous, but these characteristics were often balanced and moderated by their more restrained lawyerlike qualities. I doubt that these good qualities were as dominant as Anthony Kronman appears to think they were,[1] but they existed in conspicuous amounts in prominent lawyers in Atlanta in the sixties and seventies, and they also existed to an obvious degree in most of their law firms.

Today competitive circumstances appear to leave no room for modesty and restraint. With more good lawyers than legal work to be done, the modest lawyer does not find the world beating a path to his or her door. The failure of modesty and restraint has also been a result of the growth in the size of the profession and in the number and sizes of law firms. As the number of lawyers and law firms has increased, it has become more difficult for the public to distinguish among them. I never cease to be amazed at how little time most clients spend picking their lawyers and how many seem to rise to the bait of the best-known name. Because abandoning restraint and loudly sounding your own horn works as a tool for winning clients, more and more lawyers and firms are resorting to these tactics.

In an environment where there is not enough good work to support the collective spending habits of the major-firm lawyers, it is more difficult to be deliberative, disinterested, thoughtful, and restrained. If a client mistakes these qualities for a lack of interest, enthusiasm, and commitment to the client's cause, the client might well seek out another lawyer who is more partisan.

EARNING YOUR INCOME BY
THE SWEAT OF YOUR BROW

Keeping track of your day, day in and day out, in six-minute intervals becomes very tiresome after only a few years. There is constant pressure to fudge a bit on the figures, because every business practice firm lawyer is faced with the issue of how to produce the high number of billable hours most firms require. It is rare for a phone call or a conference to last for an amount of time that is precisely some increment of six minutes. Does the lawyer round up or down when each minute costs a client $5? Some lawyers stop at the end of the day and allocate all of their time in the office among the clients for whom they worked during the day, ignoring the many interruptions and nonbillable events that occurred. Those who try to keep track of their time find it is very easy to lose track as calls come in, faxes are received, colleagues drop by to ask a question, the voice mail light comes on, or the E-mail beeps at you. Any conscientious lawyer is bound to feel frustrated and oppressed by the system. One reason most lawyers have grown fond of long conferences is that they can justify charging big blocks of time to clients because the lawyers were engaged at the conference table on behalf of their clients whether or not their minds were fully engaged.

Lawyers I know and respect will charge two-tenths or three-tenths of an hour for a five-minute phone call, justifying the practice on the interruption of their chain of thought or the carry-forward impact of the interruption on their next project, or by rationalizing that they are really worth more on this particular project than their normal billing rate, that they probably forgot to write down some time for this client in the past, or that the firm does not charge extra for night and weekend work. Everyone knows the timekeeping system cannot work to perfection and that some approximation is required. Where does the lawyer strike the balance?

Many lawyers think that many other lawyers are aggressive about recording their time. In fact, we are all aggressive about recording our time because the system requires it. Most of us are not corrupt, but the system is corrupting. All honest and thoughtful lawyers have faced this demon, and most have opted to charge more time rather than less at least at some point in their careers. These pressures and practices inevitably undermine your sense of integrity and wear you down.

PREOCCUPATIONS AND PRESUMPTIONS OF BIG-FIRM LAWYERS

What is it that lawyers themselves are finding so objectionable about some major law firms and some of their lawyers? Many lawyers feel trapped and dependent on their firm's "rainmakers," whom they may not like or admire, to generate enough highly profitable business to maintain their high levels of income. In an article about Winston & Strawn, one of the country's best-known firms and the twenty-first largest in 1995, the firm's leading business producer, a forty-seven-year-old former U.S. attorney was quoted as saying: "I am a hustler. I'm proud I'm a hustler . . . because the best lawyer in the United States is the lawyer [who] has the best client."[2] It is not obvious why a "hustler" would necessarily have the best client or who the best client would be, but numbers speak louder than words, and this lawyer's success in generating business for his firm supports the proposition that hustling works.

In an article about Graham & James, a distinguished West Coast firm and the seventy-second largest in the United States in 1995, a partner in the Los Angeles office (where the average partner earned $296,000 a year in 1993) was concerned that the firm's San Francisco office "had free Cokes and juices," which he had calculated cost the firm "$79,000, $80,000, $90,000 a year." In his office "everyone paid for their own Coke."[3] These quotes reflect a preoccupation with money and a lack of modesty and restraint that are widespread today.

Throughout the article on Graham & James and in many other articles appearing in the legal press, the big-firm lawyers appear to be preoccupied with what they perceive to be the inadequacy of their compensation. The average partner income in the San Francisco office is described as being "stuck in the neighborhood of $220,000." Profits in the Los Angeles office are described as having "dropped in 1991 from $265,000 [per partner] to $242,000, but by 1993 had bounced back up to about $296,000." The head of the Los Angeles office laments that given the fact that the firm accepts 1,800 billable hours a year from its partners, there is a limit to the firm's profits per partner to $325,000 to $350,000 a year. The firm's managing partner says, "We could push [the billable requirement] up . . . but I don't want to do that. It's not fair to people. It's overwhelming, you lose your balance in life."[4]

The statement assumes that a lawyer billing 1,800 hours a year could lead a balanced life, while doing all of the other things lawyers have to do in order to maintain their practices. Indeed, in 1991, the partners of Graham & James adopted a statement of responsibilities in which they each pledged to work for the firm 2,500 hours a year (1,800 billable hours plus an additional 700 hours in client development, management, and administrative work) — 50 hours a week, 50 weeks a year, for 40 years. Another partner is quoted as saying, "In the past, if people didn't bill 1,800 hours, we looked at the whole gestalt. Now we look at the gestalt and say, 'Can we afford the gestalt?' "[5] Given the high average partner income the firm presently enjoys, the firm can obviously "afford the gestalt." The real issue is whether the partners want even higher incomes rather than the gestalt.

What, if anything, is wrong with these concepts and statements? The implicit assumption that these partners should expect to earn on the average an extraordinary amount of money, and much more in real dollars than their predecessors, represents a material distortion in the big-firm lawyers' worldview. Major business practice lawyers on the whole do not appear to realize how well they are compensated; they take for granted the appropriateness and the fairness of their compensation levels compared with other occupations. Many do not understand the price they pay to earn such high levels of income.

I still remember vividly an evening in the early 1970s when I found myself in line at the local McDonald's with the commanding officer of my former army reserve battalion, who was a competent lawyer in his early forties practicing by himself. As chairman of my firm's recruiting committee I was preoccupied at the time with the need to raise compensation for starting associates to $14,000 a year to attract the talent we needed. When the major asked me what was on my mind, I had the poor judgment to tell him. He blanched, told me that he had never earned as much as $14,000 in a year practicing law, and walked out without bothering to order a meal. Major business practice lawyers take a lot for granted.

Our willingness to discuss our compensation with the press and to have it broadcast to the public reflects a lack of sensitivity to real world conditions and an absorption in our own closed world. It further reflects a lack of discretion and modesty that is at odds with the demeanor of our predecessors. It also reflects a lack of common sense. To parade our very high levels of compensation for all the world and our clients to read about in the press is to invite attention that most people with good sense would think it wise to avoid.

WHICH FLAG DO WE SALUTE?

Another disturbing fact about the culture of most major business practice firms is the extent to which revenue produced for the firms has become the dominant consideration in compensating partners and determining their status within their firms. It is true that in many firms in the past some partners took advantage of the dominant collegiality and failed to do their share or overstated their contribution. The same sort of problem occurs in academic communities because of the impact of tenure on motivation and attitude. I was among the young turks at the Alston firm who in the late 1960s insisted that there be a greater relationship between contribution and compensation. I believe that contribution is an appropriate basis for compensation; where I differ with the dominant attitudes today is in my definition of contribution. Law firms could not survive if the sole criteria for making partners and compensating them were the number of billable hours they collected for their time and the amount of paying business they brought into the firm.

In addition, many of today's hotshot young partners tend to exaggerate the extent to which their own efforts have produced and served "their clients" and to underestimate the contribution of the collective enterprise called "the firm." I have experienced enough firms to know that the ability to serve well a large amount of business is dependent on establishing a network of relationships with competent colleagues and obtaining their willing cooperation. If this can be accomplished at all, it cannot be accomplished overnight. Clients do not always understand the contribution made by the firm to serving their needs, or they may assume that the necessary infrastructure can be duplicated easily elsewhere without interfering with the services they receive. Often this is not the case. In even the most supportive environment, developing a team of lawyers willing and able to provide quality, cost-effective service requires time and organizational skills that are dependent on the firm as well as on the lawyer. It also requires lawyers in the firm who are not already committed to other clients and responsibilities.

Law firms should reward their lawyers for providing high-quality legal services to clients. Clients should expect their law firms to reward the lawyers who are providing such high-quality services. However, the firms are increasingly paying their lawyers based on the number of billable hours they put in themselves and the amount of business they attract that permits other lawyers in the firm to put in billable hours.

Unfortunately, high billable hours have nothing to do with providing high-quality service to clients — indeed, they are the single greatest force working against the provision of such services. As a lawyer's hours go up beyond a reasonable point, the client is receiving the services of a tired lawyer. In many cases, the lawyer is dealing with so many matters that are competing for his best thoughts and energies that some of his clients are receiving less than full value. Increasingly, clients are seeing through the bravado and selecting lawyers who add value to the client's affairs. Regrettably, today's most important standard for determining the value of its lawyers to a firm runs counter to the interest of the firm's clients.

It is also important to note the inflexibility and the lack of tolerance in many of the major firms. They do not say that a partner's compensation must be cut if he or she fails to bill 1,800 hours a year. They say that everyone must bill at least 1,800 hours a year (or 1,900, or 2,000, or more) to remain a part of the firm. Misery loves company and does not want anyone opting out by not pursuing life in the same manner as the firm's most compulsive lawyers. Some fine lawyers who work long hours do not feel it appropriate to bill their clients for everything they do relating to the client's affairs. These people are often derisively call "baby billers" because they do not bill their clients for every bit of time put on their files by lawyers in the firm.

What personal qualities enable a law firm to provide clients with excellent services at a reasonable price? Among them are a high level of intelligence, imagination, creativity, intellectual and academic curiosity, pride in the quality of workmanship, sound judgment, organization, self-discipline, attention to detail, a desire to share knowledge, the capacity and willingness to train other lawyers, integrity, responsiveness to clients' needs, and a real concern for clients. The exercise of most of these qualities runs against the drive for billable time. A partner who stops his work to explain to an associate (or a younger partner) why something is the way it is, or to share a war story and the lesson it entails, is providing a service to the firm in training its younger lawyers. He would be dishonest if he charged a client for the time, and so would the associate if he put it on his time records.

A good lawyer ought to permit his curiosity to draw him away from the task he is pursuing for his client to explore an idea or a possibility that attracts his attention but which he cannot properly charge to his client because it is not relevant to the project at hand. He should feel that he can improve on a form because it can be done better, without having to charge the client. Consequently, a good lawyer and a fair one will take the time to explore on his own, to look back to the origins of the statute he is interpreting, to satisfy his curiosity and not charge a client for the exercise.

Not all of these activities which enrich the lawyer's and the firm's ability to serve their clients are appropriately billable to clients. They reduce billable hours. There is a powerful monetary incentive not to do them.

A recent article about Latham & Watkins, another distinguished West Coast firm and the nation's fifth largest firm in 1995, tells how it abandoned its culture to "salvage profitability."[6] When average partner profits fell from $670,000 in 1989 to $575,000 in 1990, to $515,000 in 1991, the firm jettisoned most of its most distinguishing characteristics — no lawyer layoffs, significant associate participation in management, senior associate participation in profits, near unanimous advancement of senior associates to partnership, determination of partnership compensation with a deep bow to seniority — in order to "salvage profitability." The incoming partner class at Latham & Watkins in 1992 was thought to be hard hit because their base compensation had dropped to $165,000 a year (at an average age of about 33 years).

In every firm, those partners enjoying very productive years (some because of hard work and some because of good luck) want to be paid based on their current contribution. If some lawyers are to be rewarded solely based on their current contribution, then it is difficult not to deal with everyone else on the same basis, if for no other reason than otherwise there would not be enough dollars to go around. However, if only current contribution is taken into account, then it becomes inevitable that the individual partner's position becomes less stable and more unpredictable. Those lawyers whose practices are on the rise rarely foresee a possible future interruption in their own areas of practice and have a tendency to be ruthless in their own interest to the detriment of others whose practices may have taken a downturn. Of course, in today's world they can expect to be treated the same way when their time comes to suffer a slump, as it almost certainly will. Within four years I saw the business I brought to my firm decline from $8.5 million to less than $500,000 as a result of the bankruptcy of major clients. I worked just as hard in the fourth year as in the first and provided the same quality of services to my clients throughout. Productivity and compensation do not always bear a relationship to how hard one is working.

Another story about Winston & Strawn illustrates many of the same shortcomings that affected Graham & James and Latham & Watkins. When the firm suffered a significant drop in average equity partner profits to about $400,000 in 1991, Winston & Strawn reacted by asking about twenty-five partners to leave the firm (including ten who were in their midfifties or older).[7] It is hard for most people, even executives of large businesses, to sympathize with such highly paid lawyers when they are viewed as self-seeking and self-serving mercenaries (many cultivate the image) without any redeeming public interests.

The drive to bring in paying business can become so strong that partners seek to involve their firms in matters that would have been unthinkable thirty years ago. Recently, the firm of King & Spalding brought suit against three former top managers of a national public relations firm who had left the Atlanta office to start their own firm. The problem was that one of the three was the son of retired King & Spalding partner Hughes Spalding Jr., a formerly powerful leader in the firm, the grandson of another of the firm's important figures, and the great-grandson of the founding partner, Jack J. Spalding. In due course, King & Spalding bowed out of the case but not until the situation had made the front page of the Atlanta legal press. Hughes Spalding Jr. was quoted as saying: "It sounds like the lawyer who did that didn't have all his marbles. He ought to be ashamed of himself."[8] I suspect the partner responsible for bringing in this business was more distraught about losing the opportunity to represent an important client and to earn an important fee than he was about the embarrassment to the firm.

DECLINING CIVIC LEADERSHIP

I have noted that in the past at least a part of the public-spiritedness of leading lawyers was wrapped up in the promotion of their firms and their own practices, because it was through public service more than any other available means that lawyers promoted their practices. Circumstances gave a unity to the lawyers' self-interest and the interests of the community. As a result, private practice lawyers joined important civic endeavors where their natural skills and qualities coupled with their own self-interested motivation often made them outstanding community leaders.

Today major firm lawyers in their forties and fifties are less likely to be seen in prominent civic positions. This is so because lawyers are less likely to seek such positions, as noted earlier, and because they are less frequently seen by other community leaders as having the qualities desired to provide the needed leadership. Nonetheless, lawyers continue to provide civic leadership and staff support to civic projects in an amount that is disproportionate to their numbers in the community. They do not get much credit or recognition for it, however.

ROTTEN FRUIT

Further evidence of the decline of the profession is found in the growing number of prominent lawyers who steal from their clients and their own partners. The ambition and shrewdness of these lawyers exceed their character and judgment. Many of these lawyers are significantly overworked or overachieving. They slip over the edge in due course. Can anyone be altogether in his right mind who works 250 to 300 hours a month, year in and year out? Others feel justified in taking what they feel they are entitled to, whether they are legally entitled to it or not.

The fifty-one-year-old managing partner who led Winston & Strawn from 1987 to 1993 and epitomized its bottom-line mentality was reported to the Illinois Bar Association by his firm and fired in April 1994 when it was discovered that he had been stealing from the firm in an aggregate amount of $500,000. Another Winston partner who came to the firm in a merger in 1990 was found to have defrauded Winston and his prior firm of more than $1.5 million.[9] Many sad and disturbing stories of lawyers stealing from their clients and partners are reported today. Gary Fairchild, Harvey Meyerson, Lawrence Fox, and Webster Hubbell, the former deputy attorney general of the United States, are among the most prominent examples. They are extreme manifestations of the trends of the last thirty-five years that have run amok.

Developments in the practice of law since 1960 have resulted in a new model of the major firm lawyer that is less attractive and admirable than the midcentury model. Modesty and restraint are disappearing. Self-promotion and self-interest have increased. Lawyers seem to care less about how they are viewed by their clients and by the public, and money is clearly of greater significance in determining how law is practiced and how lawyers behave.

Some lawyers are getting carried away by their own compulsiveness, greed, and self-promotion and, in the process, believing themselves to be above the law and accountable only to themselves. The public has reacted by lowering its esteem for lawyers and for the legal profession. The increasing frequency with which truly tasteless and insulting jokes are told about lawyers by respected speakers at business and public meetings, not to mention on television and radio, is further evidence that the legal profession has lost status during the last thirty-five years. The public has noticed how many lawyers behave, and the negative public reaction is affecting the entire profession.

12 Challenges for Lawyers and the Legal Profession

T he lawyers in America working for major business practice law firms are faced with challenges growing out of the transformation of the practice of law that has occurred over the past thirty-five years. They work very hard and earn a great deal of money, yet many express dissatisfaction with their situations.

For many lawyers who are now in their fifties and sixties, there is a sense of betrayal, a sense that the profession is not today what they bargained for twenty-five years ago or more when they entered law school. The decline in status of the legal profession has denied to them the high community standing they thought they would enjoy in their maturity. Being a lawyer stands as an obstacle to the full realization of their ambitions.

Most of these lawyers have profited financially from their timely entry into the profession; they have ridden the wave of growth and enjoyed far greater earnings from the practice than they ever imagined in their youth. Most are glad that they do not have to start over again, and some are looking forward to retirement or have already retired. Many feel unable to retire despite their prosperity, because their expectations and standards of living have grown with their incomes; they are trying to hold on until they are old enough to begin drawing retirement benefits. Some have thrived in the new environment — perhaps even have been leaders in bringing it about — but most lament the changes that have occurred.

Most lawyers who are under fifty have grown up in the profession within the environment characteristic of today's practice. They have always kept time, they have always been well paid, and many of them entered the profession in order to be well paid. Some also feel betrayed because the easy wealth and prominence that they had anticipated have proved to be less certain of achievement and are constantly at risk of being lost.

As the incomes of outside firm lawyers have increased, the cost of their services to clients has also increased. The increased cost of using outside legal counsel has put clients in the position where it made more economic sense for many of them to build up the quality and size of their in-house legal departments than to continue their heavy reliance on outside law firms. The cost of using outside firms become so high that the clients could raise the salaries of their in-house lawyers to levels that were sufficient to attract first-class talent throughout their legal departments and still save a lot of money.

Today a few in-house general counsel earn more than the highest paid partners in the major business practice firms, but most do not. However, stock options and corporate benefits often provide additional economic incentives to lawyers to prefer in-house jobs. In addition, working conditions in-house are often superior, and the constant pressure to bring in additional clients and work does not exist. My friends from private practice who have gone in-house as general counsel tell me that they much prefer their new roles to the ones they left.

In the 1960s the senior partners of the major firms served as general counsel to the major businesses based in their communities. These were the jobs to which young lawyers aspired; attaining these jobs was the reward they anticipated. Almost all of these jobs are now held by in-house lawyers. Increasingly, the senior partners of major firms are no longer sage general counselors and advisers but leading specialists and litigators who are called on by companies to assist with major pressing problems.

The legal profession is still in transition between reliance on outside counsel and reliance on in-house staff. The concept of inside general counsel is still evolving, with a general upgrading of standards, expectations, compensation, and status. As these jobs have grown more numerous and the quality of the lawyers holding these jobs has improved, the status of in-house lawyers has increased, not only in the profession but also in the community, and the status gap between inside and outside lawyers has shrunk. At the highest levels it has disappeared. To be general counsel of Coca-Cola or Georgia Pacific is now a higher status job, both within and outside the legal profession, than being the senior partner in one of the major firms in Atlanta, and I believe this will be increasingly true in the future.

As the inside jobs continue to attract outstanding lawyers from major firms or from other in-house assignments, the status generally will continue to increase. The in-house lawyers benefit from being more clearly removed from the mercenary legal community and the plaintiff's bar. As senior executives in their organizations, they are often encouraged to play a role in community affairs. Increasingly they are seen as the community leaders that senior partners in outside law firms used to be. The fact that Joseph R. Gladden Jr., the general counsel of Coca-Cola, is now chairman of the board of trustees of Agnes Scott College, a position held in the 1960s by Alexander P. Gaines, a senior partner in what was then Alston, Miller & Gaines, is one such example.

I believe the excess supply of talented lawyers and the growing sophistication of major purchasers of legal services will result in a reduction in profits per partner at most major firms. Some firms appear to have accepted this as inevitable. Indeed, the perennial top five firms in profits per partner over the last five years (Cravath, Wachtell, Cahill, Sullivan & Cromwell, and Davis Polk) have seen their profits per partner decline an average of 17 percent from the levels achieved in the record year 1988 and 2 percent from their 1990 levels, without any adjustment for the impact of inflation.

I believe that further declines in profits per partner will occur at many firms because of lower profit margins on the work of younger lawyers and less leverage, both of which will be a result of the continuing transition of the major firms into providers of specialized legal services. Clients using these specialized services want access to seasoned experts and do not want to pay for the work of inexperienced young attorneys at the levels they now pay, if at all. Consequently, the mix of lawyers will change. There will be a lower percentage of associates and a higher percentage of partners.

INSECURITY

The number one problem faced by major business practice firm lawyers today is the increased uncertainty about what the future holds, a problem faced by people in many other occupations as well. After three long, hard, and expensive years in law school, for which he or she may have borrowed $75,000 or more, the graduate may not be able to find a job, much less a job that would make it possible to pay off student loans and keep body and soul together.

If a job is found with a law firm, there is a poor prospect of becoming a partner. In Atlanta in recent times, 10 to 20 percent of the associates have become partners at the major business practice firms. At many major New York firms today, the percentage would be less than 10 percent. Consequently, within a very few years of graduation, many students are faced with having to find another job. Because the first job is often very well paid, there is an anxiety about finding another job that pays as well.

If an associate works extremely hard and becomes a partner, there is no certainty that he or she can remain one. The shelf life of legal specialties is not what it used to be. Having devoted ten or twenty years to a particular specialization, such as real estate, municipal bonds, or securities regulatory work, partners may find the need for their services greatly reduced by changes in the national economy, by their specialty being taken in-house, or by the bankruptcy or acquisition of a major client. Some firms will make a major effort to retread lawyers for another area of practice, some will make a minor effort, and others will immediately show them the door.

The high level of compensation enjoyed by lawyers increases the sense of insecurity. Most people are good at spending what they earn or close to it. Even if they are systematically setting aside enough for their retirement, it is difficult also to set aside monies for a premature loss of employment.

The insecurity of the private practice bar serving major business clients is increased by the competition for clients that creates the ever-present danger that an important client will be lured away by another firm. There is also the danger that the client will hire an ambitious general counsel who will want to take more work in-house or to put your part of the company's business up for competitive bidding. There are few of us with so much business that the loss of a major client will not affect our compensation, not to mention our sense of security and well-being. It could lose us our job, and without significant clients it may not be possible to find another. Corporate legal departments have not shown themselves to be more receptive to hiring unemployed lawyers in their fifties and sixties than private practice firms.

High compensation also discourages consideration of other employment opportunities. These opportunities often appear less appealing because they pay so much less than what you have been earning. Having survived on $300,000 a year, how do you know you can make it on $125,000? Few of us have the strength of character to practice living at $125,000 when we are earning $300,000.

Consequently, for the private practice attorney working for a major business practice firm, the biggest problem is an omnipresent sense of insecurity and the growing risk or reality of economic retrenchment or unemployment. This sense of insecurity adds fuel to the fire for more compensation. Higher earnings provide discretionary investment income and increase the possibility of a windfall investment that might provide a margin of safety and protection against the vicissitudes of the practice. Higher earnings increase the possibility of putting aside more money for the proverbial rainy day. But in a real sense, the higher the compensation, the greater the sense of insecurity. The higher the rise, the greater the potential fall.

OVERWORK AND EXHAUSTION

After insecurity, the biggest problems of the business practice lawyer are overwork and emotional and physical exhaustion. These problems arise not just because of long hours of work; they also are a result of the stress of handling several complicated projects simultaneously, which requires extremely careful attention to detail. These strains also result from the nature of the work. Much of what lawyers do deals with controversy; much of it involves dealing with difficult people.

The fact that lawyers are service industry professionals working for other people in a highly competitive environment also contributes to exhaustion. The great increase in the number of lawyers and the increase in competition for work have brought an end to most of the relationships where the client needed the lawyer more than the lawyer needed the client. This situation affects the way clients deal with their lawyers. Why should a client be sympathetic and understanding when a lawyer's involvement with a matter for another client prevents the lawyer from responding as rapidly as the client would like? There is another lawyer of equal competence waiting around the corner who would welcome the business and who has the time to do it now. Consequently, the private practice lawyer's life is full of pressures to perform instantly for different clients.

When they have the opportunity, lawyers are generally trying to serve more clients than they can serve comfortably or well. There is a constant fear of not having enough billable work to meet the firm's billable hour requirements. Instead of enjoying the occasional respite that even the best lawyers experience from time to time, the insufficiently occupied lawyer frets, revs up his client development activities, and instead of taking a well-earned vacation he stays at his office for fear of missing the next opportunity. Some lawyers are so consumed by worry that they work all the time and take no vacations. When they do take off a few days, they stay glued to their telephones or fax machines.

A 1984 poll of the American Bar Association showed that 41 percent of the lawyers responding would choose another profession if they had it to do over again. The Emory University School of Law recently received 1,500 applications from practicing lawyers for a handful of teaching positions. It is a well-known fact that many lawyers become alcoholics or drug addicts; this is usually attributed to an inability to deal with the stress and unpleasant aspects of the practice. It is estimated that 15 to 20 percent of practicing lawyers are alcoholics, approximately twice as high a percentage as in the general population.[1]

THE LOSS OF PROFESSIONALISM

Many of the problems faced by individual lawyers and by law firms are being addressed by the organized bar under the rubric of "professionalism." Georgia's first convocation on professionalism was held on October 14, 1988, convened by the chief justice of the Georgia Supreme Court. The program was entitled "The Practice of Law – Is There Anything More to It Than Making Money?"

This program, like many others conducted around the country, reflected the discomfort that many lawyers felt then, and that more feel today, about the circumstances under which they earn their livings.

In a speech to that convocation, Prof. Calvin Woodard of the University of Virginia Law School noted that we face a paradoxical problem in that access to our courts and to the legal system as it exists today for women, blacks, and other minorities is greater and fairer than at any time in our history. On the other hand, "We all know there is the day-to-day crisis of the conduct of other lawyers, of the way law is being practiced, and the circumstances are really appalling." Professor Woodard went on to ask, "How can it be that where law is performing socially in a very desirable way, so many people in the profession are nevertheless so dismayed by it?"[2]

The openness of the legal profession to women and minorities has increased the size and quality of the pool of available talent, which has resulted in an increase in the competition for positions for all those seeking them. The growth of the talent pool has contributed to a sense of insecurity and to growing diversity. Greatly increased competition for the highest paying jobs and for legal work, on one hand, and high compensation, on the other, have had more to do with the changes in how law is practiced and the resulting perception of a loss of professionalism than any other factors.

THE FUTURE OF MAJOR BUSINESS PRACTICE LAW FIRMS

What does the future hold for major business practice lawyers and their firms? I believe that the future remains promising for the type of lawyers who have become partners in the major firms, but the future of the major firms is less promising. I believe that more of the best lawyers will be employed in-house in the years ahead. The economic and service advantages of in-house counsel are so compelling that it is hard to imagine that many large or medium-sized companies will not use in-house legal staff as much as possible. The principal benefits to the clients of doing so are lower cost, more relevant advice, and more comprehensive and knowledgeable attention to their legal affairs.

Some businesses spending as little as $100,000 a year for regular, recurring legal services might benefit from having their own lawyer in-house. A company with only one lawyer in-house will need an experienced lawyer for that position. It is doubtful that a lawyer with only a few years of experience could effectively manage an in-house legal function. A company of any real size and sophistication would need a lawyer with significant experience to lead its legal affairs. To date, most in-house lawyers have received their training by working for a private practice firm. In the future, many of the larger legal departments will hire lawyers directly from law school and do their own training.

Most companies spending $200,000 a year for regular, recurring legal advice would benefit from bringing some of their legal work in-house. In a recent conversation with the general counsel of a national company based in Atlanta, I learned that the average cost of the legal services provided by his lawyer staff to his company was approximately $100 per hour with all appropriate related costs and benefits included. With starting rates of $110 per billable hour for new associates in Atlanta and rates of $200 an hour or more for lawyers with eight or more years of experience, this company (considering the quality and seniority of its staff) was paying less than half what it would have cost for the same services from an outside law firm, and it was being better served in the process.

The major firms in Atlanta pay starting associates $60,000 a year or about $30 to $35 an hour for billable work, which is charged to the client at $110. A young partner earning $150,000 a year, billing 1,800 hours a year, earns about $83 an hour ($75 an hour if he or she bills 2,000 hours a year), which is billed to the client at $200 an hour or more. Although the firms have to pay for their significant overhead out of these revenues, the fees billed to clients for the work of associates and younger partners are more than sufficient to cover the overhead and to provide a significant profit. The markup accounts for a substantial part of the income of the law firms' partners. By bringing the work in-house, the client avoids the markup and the law firm partners lose the benefit of it.

From the point of view of the clients served by in-house counsel, the advantages are not limited to cost savings. The clients get broader and better service. Unless they have retainer relationships, clients know that every time they pick up the phone to call their outside law firm it will cost additional money. There is a reluctance to do so unless the need is significant. Consequently, there are many questions that would benefit from some legal input but do not receive it. Forms and small contracts are done without any legal assistance. People do not ask questions because of costs, or because they have to get permission from a superior before talking with the company's outside lawyer, or because they do not know the outside lawyer well enough to trust him. Such obstacles are reduced or eliminated if legal counsel is available in-house and, as a result, legal advice can be brought to bear on issues more easily. The lawyers I know who served clients as outside general counsel before moving in-house tell me that they are serving their clients better in-house than they did from the outside.

WHAT WORK IS LEFT TO DO?

What sort of legal work will remain available to the major business practice firms? Company legal departments will still need the assistance of outside lawyers to provide specialized knowledge or skills not available among their in-house lawyers. One reason why the major firms are marketing their services all over the country is that there is not enough demand in local markets for specialized legal services to support even a small department of high-quality specialists. Consequently, most of the major firms are trying to broaden the markets for their services, a trend that is converting the United States and the entire world into one large market for legal services. It is not yet clear whether or not it will be possible for large local or regional firms to survive against such national and international competition.

Company legal departments will also need the assistance of outside firms to staff major projects. It does not make sense for a company to have an environmental lawyer on its staff if environmental problems arise only occasionally. It will also not make sense for a company to staff its legal department to handle major but occasional matters such as mergers and acquisitions or major litigation. Consequently, there will be a continuing need for the services of outside specialists to assist with major transactions and litigation.

Litigators are here to stay and will be the foundation of the practice of any major firm. Many of the specialties that have remained vigorous in outside law firms have a strong litigation component to them. Labor, government contracts, antitrust, and intellectual property are examples. The result is that the litigation or quasi-litigation component of the major firms has generally increased over the past thirty-five years.

Newly developing specialties generally will be staffed outside before they are staffed inside. Many specialties become commodity services over time and are taken in-house when a business needs the service on a regular basis. Much of the corporate and securities regulatory work that was once a staple of major business practice firms is an example of legal services that have become commodities.

Some major businesses with enough legal work to support a specialist in a particular area nonetheless forgo the opportunity because they are receiving good service from their outside lawyers and at an acceptable price. The savings that could be realized by bringing the service in-house may not be enough to cause the change at this time, but as the outside lawyers involved in these historical relationships begin to retire, some of this work will move in-house.

Another reason clients use many of the larger business practice firms is that most of these firms have an office in Washington,

D.C., staffed with former government lawyers who enjoy good relations with their former colleagues and daily working contact with important government agencies. It is not cost-effective for any but the largest individual businesses to set up Washington law offices and hire such lawyers. It is no accident that fifty-seven of the sixty largest firms in the country and all six of the major Atlanta firms have offices in Washington.

Another type of legal work available to outside firms is some of the legal work of businesses like investment banks and other financial institutions, which have legal staffs to deal with recurring matters but which usually use outside lawyers to represent them in financing transactions. Because the size of the legal fees involved in major transactions is usually a small part of the total transaction cost, there is often less pressure in these transactions to reduce the legal bills. In addition, the client's customer usually pays the client's lawyers.

The public offering business of investment banking firms is notoriously cyclical, so it has made sense for the investment banks not to have in-house the legal personnel necessary to do this work. In addition, the referral potential of law firms is so great that investment banks benefit from using outside lawyers, who in return steer the business of their clients to the banks.

A recent survey of the American Corporate Counsel Association found that more than three-quarters of the respondents had not recently outsourced significant work. About a third indicated that they had retained outside counsel for between 26 and 50 percent of their work, primarily litigation. Other specialties in demand were employment benefits, mergers and acquisitions, tax, intellectual property, and commercial matters.[3]

What else is there for outside firms to do? A major area of opportunity is the work of smaller businesses that use less than $100,000 – $200,000 worth of regular, recurring legal services a year. Many of the major law firms have given up the pursuit of this type of business because they think that they cannot do it at the level of profitability to which they have grown accustomed. This is the work that keeps many smaller to medium-sized law firms busy, along with litigation. I believe that major firms based in cities like Atlanta can service some of this business profitably if they set their minds to providing cost-effective service.

Most of the major firms that have thought seriously about their future are moving to maintain their profitability and viability by becoming national providers of specialized legal services. These firms are trying to create national networks of offices serving large parts of the country. Through these offices they are marketing the types of services that are now the staples of major firm practice in the 1990s: specialty services, major transaction and litigation services, and services to investment banking and other financial institutions. The competition for these types of representations is growing increasingly intense because most of the major business practice firms are pursuing this work all over the country. The average number of domestic offices for the 60 largest firms is 6.15. Hinshaw & Culbertson of Chicago has 17 offices, and LeBoeuf, Lamb, Greene & McRae L.L.P. of New York has 13. More of the 60 largest firms have offices in Washington, D.C., than in any other city (57). The next most popular location is New York (49), followed by Los Angeles (34), Chicago (16), San Francisco (13), Miami (10), and Dallas, Denver, and Houston (9). The 27 largest firms in the country all have offices in Washington, D.C., 24 have offices in New York City, and 21 have offices in California.

In addition to opening offices in several important cities, many of the larger firms have gotten much more aggressive about marketing their services in parts of the country where they do not have offices. A recent survey revealed that over a thirteen-month period ending May 31, 1995, ninety Georgia-based companies made public offerings of their securities. Fifty-six of these offerings were handled for the issuer by Georgia-based legal counsel or Atlanta offices of national firms. However, thirty-four of these companies used other legal counsel, and fourteen used New York counsel. Of twenty-seven Georgia-based companies that went public during the same period, six used New York counsel, and five used other nonsouthern counsel.[4]

Twenty years ago, these Georgia companies would not have

considered using firms located outside the state to do this work. These assignments are a result of the significant effort by many of the major firms to market their services beyond the boundaries of their traditional markets. Most of these firms have used their relationships with major investment banking or venture capital firms to secure these representations. Major business practice firms based in Atlanta can no longer assume that their principal competition comes from similar firms in Atlanta. The competition is now nationwide, not just for Atlanta-based firms but for firms throughout the country.

A nationwide growth strategy will work for some firms, but it cannot work for all. The point of such a strategy is to grow by taking business away from regional firms and other major firms. As a result, some firms will lose market share to out-of-area competitors or more successful in-area competitors and will be forced out of business.

Some major firms are looking to international growth to maintain and increase their business and profitability. A recent article in the *American Lawyer* compares the strategy of three of the nation's most important law firms: Cravath Swaine & Moore; Sullivan & Cromwell; and Davis Polk & Wardwell.[5] All three of these firms see international expansion as an aspect of their future growth and prosperity, but some much more than others. Over 12 percent of Sullivan & Cromwell's lawyers work overseas in the firm's six foreign offices; 10 percent of Davis Polk's lawyers work in the firm's five foreign offices. Five percent of Cravath's lawyers are stationed in its two foreign offices. Although Cravath is concentrating more on domestic growth than the others, it is the only law firm among the sixty largest in the United States with only one U.S. office.

I believe the in-house segment of the legal profession will continue to grow, and the large firms will continue to evolve into multiservice specialty boutiques. I do not think that it will be possible for all of the major business practice firms to survive as specialty boutiques, and most will not be successful as providers of legal services to smaller businesses. It is difficult to contain within a single law firm the attitudes and skills needed to cultivate these disparate markets.

Some firms will lose ground and will be forced to reduce the compensation of their lawyers in order to compete on costs, or they will disappear altogether. Some will wake up to their dilemma too late, will be unable to claim a place in one or the other of the surviving modes, and will find the cost of getting competitive too high and the lead time required too great to get back into the running. They will find some of their best lawyers with the best books of business moving to the firms that have the strongest competitive positions and can pay the highest salaries. Strong firms will become even stronger in the process.

A few firms will be able to continue in the present mode. These firms are already providing the specialized services and major project support that is periodically required by large corporate legal departments. Faced with large and complex business transactions, some management will want the feeling of having bought the best legal services available even at the cost of extravagant legal bills. Like expensive perfume, cost is seen by some as the indicium of quality. Unfortunately for many of the major firms, there are not enough of these transactions to go around.

Is it possible for some major business practice firms to become so efficient that they can win back business that has gone in-house by providing service at a lower price than the cost of the in-house legal department? I think this is very unlikely. The economic advantages of in-house legal departments for large and medium-sized companies are so strong that I think the in-house segment of the legal profession will continue to grow.

There will also be experimentation with outsourcing some of the business that has been taken in-house, particularly where it can be done on a fixed fee basis. Some major firms are agreeing to do such work for a fixed fee. This could be the result of increased efficiencies that will maintain the profitability of the firms doing it, or the firms may expect a reduction in their profitability but prefer that to reducing their lawyer workforce. The recent arrangement between ALCOA and LeBoeuf, Lamb is an example of one or the other.[6]

I doubt that all six large Atlanta-based firms, or all twenty or more of the large New York–based firms, will have sufficient management and marketing skills to compete successfully in the markets available to them and to maintain even their recent level of prosperity. Indeed, the Atlanta firms have accomplished something of a minor miracle by increasing their profits per partner over the last five years despite a small decline in their associate leverage. I wish it were possible to predict that the major business practice firms could continue on their recent course of profitability without interruption, but I do not think that will happen.

I expect that many major firms will adjust the way in which they allocate their reduced profits among their partners, with the rainmakers' share increasing. Other firms may burn themselves out in a frenzied effort to push everyone still harder to maintain current levels of profitability. Major firms with distinguished histories will continue to wither and die because of inadequate clientele and insufficient revenue to pay their rainmakers enough to keep them on board and to cover their other costs. Many are saddled with elaborate facilities and expensive leases that they might prefer not to have at this time.

As in every other profession and in business, there will be miscalculations and misjudgments that will cause strong firms to lose their lead and enable aggressive and able competitors to take their place. In the process, clients will be better served, and the value of the services they receive will rise relative to their costs. As in most other things, the race will go to those with the most talent who have made the greatest and smartest effort.

ASLEEP AT THE SWITCH

The law schools have slept through this revolution. For the most part they have not paid any attention to how law firms function and how legal services are delivered to clients; they have focused only on the letter of the law itself and on how it is interpreted by the courts. As a result, the law schools are not in a position to inform their students about the great transformation that has occurred in the practice of law in America or to assist the profession in understanding and addressing these sweeping changes. Most law school graduates enter the profession without any understanding of how law practice economics have reshaped and are reshaping the legal profession, the practice of law, and the legal system in this country. Most law school professors get their practical training from a few years with a private practice firm, and they know very little about the practice of law in private firms or in-house. Traditionally, law schools have not thought it important to pay attention to what was going on in these areas.

The law schools have an obligation to their students, the legal profession, and the American public to study how the legal world works economically and financially and to help the legal profession find constructive ways in which to deal with its problems. These problems affect the way the American legal system serves the public. Without such help I think it will be difficult, if not impossible, for the profession to correct its course for the better and for the public to be better served by our legal system.

IS THERE MORE TO THE PRACTICE OF LAW THAN EARNING MONEY?

There are still important differences among law firms with respect to their attitudes toward working conditions, compensation, quality of legal service, professionalism, the meaning of partnership, and community service. I know from personal experience that some law firms value the qualities that make a lawyer a better lawyer more highly than others. It is clear that there is more pressure in some firms than in others to bill time and to skimp on the rest. There are firms where you can call a colleague to discuss an issue for a couple of minutes, and the lawyer on the other end of the line does not ask to which file he should bill his time. There are others where you initiate such a conversation, and the other lawyer wants the file and billing number before the conversation commences. There are firms where you ask a colleague for assistance on a matter outside your area of competence, and he asks you how much of the origination credit and responsibility credit he will get if he takes it on. There are other firms where such assistance is readily given — no questions asked.

A recent article about the firm of Debevoise & Plimpton (the nation's fifty-third largest in 1995 and ninth in profits per partner for 1994) is reassuring in that the firm appears to have been able to practice law the old-fashioned way and to put the firm culture above dollars. This New York–based firm of 349 lawyers (down from 360 in 1993) did not lay off associates or partners to compensate for a decline in profits per partner from $655,000 in 1989, to $635,000 in 1991, to $560,000 in 1992.[7] They maintained their lock-step compensation system for partners and modified their management structure only slightly. By 1994, profits per partner had rebounded to $805,000.[8] The rebound may explain the lack of change, or vice versa.

How does a law firm decide what it wants its culture to be, and how can that be measured and maintained? Short-term financial results are easy to measure and to compare among lawyers and firms (assuming the type of information published by the legal press is correct). Lifestyles and practice styles are a much more personal matter. What is perfectly acceptable for one person is not for another. How can these differences be accommodated?

It is clearly easier to do in a relatively small organization where the partners know one another and most of them have been together for a long time. It helps if they are friends. It helps if they are all working in the same office. As firms grow larger, as they bring in lateral partners and associates, as they open branches in their city or in other cities, there is an inevitable weakening of the bonds of familiarity and friendship that erodes the nonfinancial ties. In this way, the institutionalization of the large firms is a liability.

When the standard of obligation to the firm in terms of hours and commitment becomes so high that the lawyers' private lives are significantly and adversely affected, as has happened almost everywhere, concerns about compensation usually increase, and tolerance for differences among the partners usually declines. Consequently, as firms have grown larger and more diverse, as they have opened offices in other cities, and as the demands on the lawyers have increased, considerations of firm culture have declined in importance, and compensation has become increasingly important.

I think it is unlikely that the trends discussed in this book will be reversed. I think the legal profession will see even larger national and international law firms in the years ahead. Competition (including growing in-house capability) will continue to put a downward pressure on profits per partner until the average income of major firm lawyers comes more into line with economic reality. Although I think the profits per partner will decline, I believe that those partners who are successful in marketing their firms' services will demand and receive a higher percentage of the firm's profits than in the past and they will be very well rewarded.

Clients will become more sophisticated about the quality and costs of legal services and will direct more of their work to firms that provide greater value. They will be more likely to find that value at firms that are not highly leveraged, that are well managed, that prize client service a little more and profit a little less, and that maintain high standards. Some firms will make a serious effort to become competitive on a cost-effective basis and will benefit from doing so. As average compensation declines, other things will come back into better balance, and some of the qualities long associated with the profession may come back into favor.

We know how difficult it is to reform any large institution, as is evidenced by the difficulty encountered in changing the main programs of the federal government. The American legal system is also entrenched in its ways, and many people who profit from the status quo seek to preserve it with an energy that far exceeds the zeal of most reformers. Nevertheless, if the legal service delivery system is not reformed, the cost of legal services and the burden of the law on the national economy can only increase.

Cost containment initiatives by clients have caused many of the major business practice firms to start thinking about some of these issues, and some savvy lawyers and law firms have figured out that offering cost-effective services can give them a competitive edge. But as long as the prevailing styles of practice are as profitable as they are, lawyers and law firms will not be the source of major reform. Indeed, any reform that reduces the need for so many highly paid lawyers runs contrary to the interests of this group, and they will oppose it. Meanwhile the burdens of the system's wasteful practices oppress business clients who pay for them, and ultimately the public suffers as well.

The public's awareness of the excesses in the legal profession and the public's growing disdain for lawyers may eventually cause the legal profession to seek to improve its image through self-reform. Many lawyers are demoralized by the atmosphere of waste, greed, and vicious competition in which they must spend their working lives. If a golden past ever existed, when lawyers were admired and respected for their integrity, discipline, and restraint, we have a long way to travel to get back to that professional environment. It would be worth the trip.

NOTES

PREFACE

1. In 1963 the firm changed its name to Alston, Miller & Gaines. As a result of a merger with the Atlanta firm of Jones, Bird & Howell in 1982, the firm became known as Alston & Bird.

2. "The NLJ 250: Annual Survey of the Nation's Largest Law Firms," *National Law Journal*, 9 October 1995, C10.

3. The bank, subsequently named C&S/Sovran, merged with North Carolina's NCNB, forming NationsBank.

4. Jill Abramson, "Getting in on the Ground Floor," *American Lawyer*, April 1982, 39.

5. "At Issue: Associate Leveraging, a Formula for Disaster," *American Bar Association Journal*, February 1992, 36; "Cut Pay, and Later, Firms Will Do Better," *National Law Journal*, 19 July 1993, 13; "How Firms Trapped Themselves," *National Law Journal*, 16 November 1992, 13; "Law Practice Satisfaction: A Modest Proposal," *Georgia Journal of Southern Legal History* 2, nos. 1&2 (1993): 253. The author notes that the titles of the articles were selected by the publications.

INTRODUCTION

1. According to information supplied by the American Bar Association statistics department.

2. "The NLJ 250," *National Law Journal*, 9 October 1995. Revenue figures for 1994 are from "The Am Law 100" survey, *American Lawyer*, July/August 1995. Subsequent information in this book concerning size and locations, and profits per partner, in 1995 and 1994, respectively, are from the same sources.

3. Deborah L. Arron, *Running from the Law*, (Berkeley, Calif.: Ten Speed Press, 1991); *Broken Contract: A Memoir of Harvard Law School* (New York: Hill and Wang, 1992); Richard W. Moll, *The Lure of the Law* (New York: Viking, 1990).

4. In Georgia, for instance, the first annual convocation on professionalism was held in 1988, convened by the chief justice of the Georgia Supreme Court in conjunction with the state bar.

5. Sol M. Linowitz, *The Betrayed Profession: Lawyering at the End of the Twentieth Century* (New York: Scribner, 1994); Anthony T. Kronman, *The Lost Lawyer: Failing Ideals of the Legal Profession* (Cambridge, Mass.: Belknap Press, 1993).

CHAPTER ONE: THE PRACTICE OF LAW IN 1960

1. The Crenshaw, Hansell firm merged with Moise, Post & Gardner in 1962 and changed its name to Hansell, Post, Brandon & Dorsey. It then changed its name to Hansell & Post in 1982. In 1989, Hansell & Post merged with the national law firm Jones, Day, Reavis & Pogue, becoming its Atlanta office.

2. Unless otherwise indicated, historical statistics concerning firm size, composition, and location are derived from the appropriate annual volume of *The Martindale-Hubbell Law Directory* (New York: Martindale-Hubbell; Chicago: Reed).

3. Smith, Kilpatrick, Cody, Rogers & McClatchey, which was known by that name until 1964 when it became Kilpatrick, Cody, Rogers, McClatchey & Regenstein. In 1980, the name of the firm was shortened to its present incarnation, Kilpatrick & Cody.

4. The category "counsel" encompasses several titles, including "of counsel" and "special counsel." The status of attorneys listed in these categories varies from firm to firm and from year to year. For instance, "of counsel" often refers to a semiretired or retired member of a firm, whereas "counsel" may be an intermediate step between associate and partner. In other firms, "counsel" may refer to a senior lateral hire who has not been admitted to the partnerships, and in still others, it encompasses both meanings. Some firms, particularly in later years, introduced an intermediate category known as "senior attorney." The lawyers listed under this heading have been included in associate counts. Because senior attorneys or associates do not commonly take draws from firm income, this method of counting is defensible in most cases. Of course, if participation in firm profits is the sine qua non of partnership, then it might be suggested that nonequity partners – a tier of partnership introduced in the late 1980s – should also be counted among the associates. Not wanting to beg or dodge the question, but recognizing that *Martindale-Hubbell* does not indicate partnership tiers, this book will limit itself to partners, associates, and counsel.

5. In 1972, the firm became Troutman, Sanders, Lockerman & Ashmore. The name was shortened to Troutman Sanders in 1993.

6. "At Issue: Associate Leveraging, a Formula for Disaster," *American Bar Association Journal*, February 1992, 36.

7. The Alston firm created a litigation department in 1968.

8. Jean Curry Allen was asked by the Crenshaw, Hansell firm to come on board as an associate in 1953 to handle residential real estate closing work. Although she "had some misgivings about limiting myself to such a confined area," she accepted and became a partner in 1958. Harvey H.

Jackson, *Hansell & Post: From King & Anderson to Jones, Day, Reavis & Pogue* (Atlanta: Hansell & Post, 1989), 123 – 25.

9. Antha Mulkey was a secretary for Hughes Spalding of the firm then known as Spalding, Sibley, Troutman & Brock until she became an associate in 1942. Della Wager Wells, *The First Hundred Years: A Centennial History of King & Spalding* (Atlanta: King & Spalding, 1985), 172 – 74.

10. Faye A. Hankin and Duane W. Krohnke, *The American Lawyer: 1964 Statistical Report* (Chicago: American Bar Foundation, 1965), 29.

11. There was a professional bias against in-house counsel in those days. As Lea Agnew and Jo Ann Haden-Miller noted in their history of the Atlanta Bar Association: "Lawyers working as in-house counsel were deemed a strange breed for many years. The Atlanta Bar Association did not recognize them as 'practicing' lawyers and put them in a special 'associate' membership category." *Atlanta and Its Lawyers: A Century of Vision, 1888 – 1988* (Atlanta: Atlanta Bar Association, 1988), 91.

CHAPTER TWO: ECONOMIC GROWTH — DYNAMIC CHANGE

1. According to Dr. Harvey H. Jackson, author of *Hansell & Post: From King & Anderson to Jones, Day, Reavis & Pogue* (Atlanta: Hansell & Post, 1989), the Hansell firm "entered the decade of the 1980s with a force of one hundred and forty-one attorneys, sixty-two of whom were partners." Dr. Jackson's figures cannot be reconciled with the *Martindale-Hubbell* counts for 1979, 1980, or 1981. It should be noted that the discrepancy may result from *Martindale-Hubbell*'s practice of not listing new associates or lateral hires from other states who have not passed the bar by the reporting deadline. With justification, the bar associations do not look with pleasure upon the listing of lawyers who are not authorized to practice law in the jurisdiction. As a result, comparative differences exist between the directory and other sources. However, this practice is unlikely to explain the significant differences in the Hansell firm lawyer count in 1980.

2. If *Martindale-Hubbell* is to be credited, the average ratio of associate leverage for the group of seven in 1980 was 1.05:1. If Dr. Jackson's larger figure for the Hansell firm is correct, the ratio would be 1.12:1.

3. Lea Agnew and Jo Ann Haden-Miller, *Atlanta and Its Lawyers: A Century of Vision, 1888 – 1988* (Atlanta: Atlanta Bar Association, 1988), 170.

4. The Atlanta office of Jones, Day is included with the six major firms based in Atlanta.

5. Agnew and Haden-Miller, *Atlanta and Its Lawyers*, 170.

6. Letter from James M. Sibley to author, 21 March 1990.

7. See the *Directory of Legal Employers, 1991* (Washington: National Association of Law Placement, 1991).

8. Expressed in salary comparisons, new associate compensation of $14,000 a year in 1970 would have to be increased to about $27,700 in 1980 in order to keep pace with inflation. New associate compensation — in Atlanta, at least — had only reached $24,000 in 1980.

9. Again put in terms of salary comparisons, new associate pay of $24,000 a year in 1980 would have to be increased to $41,000 in 1990 to maintain the same buying power: a 71 percent increase. New associate salaries had actually reached $60,000 by 1990, an increase of 150 percent.

10. Personal records of Michael H. Trotter.

11. Statistical information with respect to inflation was taken from "Consumer Price Indexes, 1960 – 1993," in the *Statistical Abstract of the United States, 1994* (Washington: Department of Commerce, September 1994), 488; "Consumer Price Index," in the *Labor Relations Expediter* (Washington: Bureau of National Affairs, 1995), LRX 430:701. Please note that because the inflation in one decade compounds the inflation for the prior decades, you cannot add up the inflation rate in each period to get the cumulative inflation for the thirty-five-year period.

12. In determining inflation, I calculated the inflation for the decades as follows: 1960 – 1969, 1970 – 1979, and 1980 – 1989 rather than 1961 – 1970, 1971 – 1980, and 1981 – 1990. Because inflation reached a high of 13.5 percent in 1980, its placement in the calculation makes a significant difference.

13. *A Review of Legal Education in the United States, Fall of 1994* (Chicago: American Bar Association, Section of Legal Education and Admissions to the Bar, 1995), 67.

14. "The NLJ 250," *National Law Journal*, 9 October 1995, C6 – C21.

15. According to listings from the 1990 *Martindale-Hubbell*. The 1989 directory listed 143 attorneys in the firm, reflecting a 38 percent drop after the merger. The 1994 directory lists 76 lawyers. *National Law Journal*'s 9 October 1995 report lists 90.

CHAPTER THREE: THE PRACTICE OF LAW IN THE 1990S

1. "The Am Law 100 – Ranked by Profits per Partner," *American Lawyer*, July/August 1995, 55.

2. Jonathan Ringel, "Sutherland Slashes N.Y. Office," *Fulton County Daily Report*, 30 October 1995, 1.

3. "The NLJ 250," *National Law Journal*, 9 October 1995, C6 – C21. The figures were projected to be accurate as of 30 September, 1995. Any variance between *Martindale-Hubbell* and the NLJ 250 survey is likely caused by two factors: the difference in reporting deadlines, and the fact that *Martindale-Hubbell* does not count lawyers who have not passed the bar, whereas the *National Law Journal* survey does. Unfortunately, the *NLJ* has compiled data only since 1978. For a fuller exposition on the difficulties of historical firm size research, see Marc Galanter and Thomas Palay, *Tournament of Lawyers: The Transformation of the Big Law Firm* (Chicago: University of Chicago Press, 1991), app. A.

4. These figures exclude Jones, Day attorneys in other cities (which would double the total!), and they exclude Sutherland's Washington office. The figures do include a relatively small number of lawyers at branch offices in other cities. This margin of error is caused by differences in format of *Martindale-Hubbell* entries. King & Spalding, for instance, listed its attorneys resident in Washington with its Atlanta office in 1990. In 1994, the New York and Washington offices were listed separately from the Atlanta office. This change reflects increased size and importance of the branch offices.

5. "Firm Listings," *National Law Journal*, 27 September 1993. As noted above, *Martindale-Hubbell* does not distinguish nonequity from participating partners.

6. The figures for African Americans for 1990 include Sutherland's Washington office but exclude Jones, Day altogether (this was when Hansell & Post was making the transition to a Jones, Day branch office). The figures are from Rita Henley Johnson, "Minorities Didn't Share in Firm Growth," *National Law Journal*, 19 February 1990, 1.

7. According to the LEXIS service's *Employer Directory*, and now including Jones, Day's Atlanta office, but excluding Sutherland's Washington office. The total number of African American partners in significant Atlanta firms including, but not limited to, the seven oldest and largest was estimated to be no more than twenty-four by Marva Jones Brooks, partner at Arnall, Golden & Gregory and past president of the Gate City Bar Association, Atlanta's African American bar association. Don J. DeBenedictus, "Changing Faces: Coming to Terms with Growing Minority Populations," *American Bar Association Journal*, April 1991, 55.

8. Classifying counsel and senior attorneys as associates and including the Atlanta office of Jones, Day.

9. Profitability being determined by profits per partner. "The Am Law 100 – Ranked by Profits per Partner," *American Lawyer*, July/August 1995. Supp. 55.

10. See Della Wager Wells, *The First Hundred Years: A Centennial History of King & Spalding* (Atlanta: King & Spalding, 1985), 182.

11. Elbert Tuttle of Sutherland, Tuttle & Brennan was president of the Atlanta Chamber of Commerce in 1949, and Francis "Buster" Bird of Jones, Bird & Howell presided in 1957.

CHAPTER FOUR: COMPENSATION

1. *A Review of Legal Education in the United States – Fall 1994* (Chicago: American Bar Association, Section of Legal Education and Admissions to the Bar, 1995).

2. This included a $12,000 housing allowance. The salary was quickly matched by dozens of New York firms. Stewart Yerton, "The Years in Review: 1986," *American Lawyer*, March 1994, 76.

3. All information on partner income at the major Atlanta firms prior to 1986 is based on the author's private survey and personal records.

4. Information based on the annual survey of the top ten firms in Atlanta, first published in 1986 by the *Fulton County Daily Report*.

5. Based on the "Am Law 100" survey of the *American Lawyer* for each year in question.

6. This sample includes banks, insurers, diversified financial services companies, transportation companies, and manufacturers.

7. This sum includes benefits but excludes long-term compensation plans, which have no clear analog in law firm partner compensation.

8. "What Lawyers Earn – Partners at Large Firms," *National Law Journal*, 30 May 1994, supp. C4.

9. The average age of the fifty-four partners of Wachtell, Lipton, Rosen & Katz, the most profitable major business practice firm in the country in 1994, was 45.5 years. The profits per partner for the year were $1.4 million, according to the "Am Law 100" survey of the *American Lawyer*. A partner of the average age would not necessarily have been paid the average profits per partner. It is likely that the compensation scale is weighted more heavily at the senior level.

10. "What Lawyers Earn – General Counsel," *National Law Journal*, 10 July 1995, supp. C10.

CHAPTER FIVE: WORKING CONDITIONS

1. See *1991 Directory of Legal Employers, 1991* (Washington: National Association for Law Placement, 1991). Most of the New York firms that responded to the question about billable hours indicated average associate billable hours of 1,800 to 2,000, though some admitted that the average billable hours of their associates the year before had been in excess

of 2,000, and a few admitted to over 2,100. Half of the ten most profitable firms found it convenient not to answer the question. Many firms said that the average number of working hours in excess of billable hours were 50 to 100 hours a year, or less than two hours each week for administrative work, legal education, and other nonbillable working hours. The author finds such figures to be most improbable. Some firms reported the spread between total working hours and billable hours to be in the range of 200 to 500 hours a year, which are much more realistic numbers. In the *1994 Directory of Legal Employers*, eight of the ten most profitable New York firms did not answer the question about billable hours. In response to a question concerning average total associate billable hours, many firms responded "not applicable," which seems disingenuous, to say the least.

2. Amy Stevens, "Top Chapman & Cutler Partner Chalked Up Astronomical Hours," *Wall Street Journal*, 27 May 1994, sec. B.

3. Nancy D. Holt, "Are Longer Hours Here to Stay?" *American Bar Association Journal*, February 1993, 62.

CHAPTER SIX: WHERE DID ALL OF THAT BILLABLE TIME COME FROM?

1. Darlene Ricker, "Greed, Ignorance, and Overbilling," *American Bar Association Journal*, August 1994, 64.

2. William G. Ross, "The Ethics of Hourly Billing," *Rutgers Law Review* 44 (fall 1991): app. Specifically, 29 percent believed such abuses occur rarely, 45.1 percent thought they occurred occasionally, and 13.7 percent responded that such practices occurred frequently.

CHAPTER SEVEN: THE NEW WAVE PRACTICE OF LAW

1. Mike France, "Reengineer Your Lawyers," *Forbes ASAP*, 6 June 1994, 55.

2. 488 A.2d 858 (1985).

3. 969 F.2d 744 (1992), rev'd on other grounds, No. 93–489 (S.Ct. June 13, 1994).

4. See chapter 10 for further analysis of the errors in this case.

5. Amy Stevens, "Suit over Suicide Raises Issue: Do Associates Work Too Hard?" *Wall Street Journal*, 15 April 1994, B1, B4.

6. Roger Parloff, "Overbilled by $57 Million?!" *American Lawyer*, May 1994, 65.

CHAPTER EIGHT: CHANGING PRACTICE STYLES AND STRATEGIES

1. The buyer's legal counsel declined to comment on the performance of the seller's counsel; the transaction, unsurprisingly, had ended up in litigation. D. M. Osborne, "Susan Pravda Pushes the Limits of Opportunity," *American Lawyer*, January 1990, 80.

2. Both the Model Rules of Professional Conduct, specifically Rule 3.3(a)(3), and the Model Code of Professional Responsibility, DR 7-106(B)(1), require attorneys to disclose authority adverse to their position to the tribunal. Omitting to correct a mistake may be the equivalent of an unethical affirmative misrepresentation. Rule 3.3, Comment 2. Obviously, total candor is required when the lawyer's client is perpetrating a fraud upon the court. Rule 3.3(a)(2); DR-102(A)(7).

3. Lawyers may not willfully misrepresent any material fact or law to opposing parties or third persons. Rule 4.1(a); Rule 8.4(c); DR 7-102(A)(5); DR 7-102(A)(4).

4. Charles Longstreet Weltner, "On with the Old!" *Georgia State Bar Journal* 24 (August 1987): 13, 17.

5. Steve Weinberg, "Hardball Discovery," *American Bar Association Journal*, November 1995, 66.

CHAPTER NINE: REFORMING THE DELIVERY OF LEGAL SERVICES

1. See "Symposium: Applying Quality Management Concepts to the Law," *Emory Law Journal* 43, (spring 1994): 394 – 533.

2. See "Special Report – The Case against Mergers," *Business Week*, 30 October 1995, 122, 124, which states in part that: "mergers and acquisitions, at least over the past 35 years or so, have hurt more than helped companies and shareholders. . . . Most of the '90s deals still haven't worked. Of 150 recent deals valued at $500 million or more, about half destroyed shareholder wealth, judged by stock performance."

3. Karen Dillon, "Can the Profession Save Itself?" *American Lawyer*, November 1994, 5, 93.

4. John E. Morris, "Two Pioneers Make a Fixed-Fee Deal Work," *American Lawyer*, December 1993, 5.

CHAPTER TEN: REFORMING THE LEGAL SYSTEM

1. To be more precise with respect to the federal judge count, there were 649 "authorized" district court judgeships in 1992. The ever-

lengthening process of nomination, Senate confirmation, and appointment invariably means that the authorized number of federal trial judges will exceed the actual number who are hearing cases. Unfortunately, given the disparity among the state court systems and the complexity of some of those arrangements, precision in counting the total number of state trial judges is not possible. The number 12,000 includes general jurisdiction courts only. Most states have lower-level courts of limited jurisdiction that can try petty criminal matters and civil actions of small value; these have been excluded. Many general jurisdiction courts can only try matters of a minimum dollar amount, despite their name, and in some states, civil and criminal trials are held in separate courts. See generally *Want's Federal-State Court Directory, 1994 Edition* (Washington: Want, 1993).

2. The Court of Veterans Appeals and the Court of Military Appeals are two examples of special courts.

3. The Office of Hearings and Appeals of the Social Security Administration and the National Labor Relations Board, for instance.

4. Thomas E. Baker, "Judges, Heal Thyselves: The Dawn of F.3d," *Legal Times*, 7 March 1994, 30.

5. "Roscoe Pound Kindles the Spark of Reform," *American Bar Association Journal*, April 1971, 35.

6. Richard C. Reuben, "New Cites for Sore Eyes," *American Bar Association Journal*, June 1994, 22.

7. Richard L. Abel, *American Lawyers* (New York: Oxford University Press, 1989), 172.

8. The statistic is from the Institute for Civil Justice at the RAND Corporation.

9. Barry M. Hartman, *Environmental Litigation: Remarks*, ALI-ABA Course of Study: Environmental Law (Chicago: American Law Institute; American Bar Association 1992), 567.

10. See Philip Howard, *The Death of Common Sense: How Law Is Suffocating America* (New York: Random House, 1994). The attitude of modern legislators toward the courts as a resource for the solution of political problems manifests itself in other ways. Pennsylvania senator Arlen Specter's recent lawsuit against the secretary of the navy for the closure of a Philadelphia shipyard pursuant to Congress's 1990 base-closing scheme and the senator's consequent appearance before the Supreme Court underscore this new trend.

11. Anthony T. Kronman, *The Lost Lawyer: Failing Ideals of the Legal Profession* (Cambridge, Mass.: Belknap Press, 1993), 348.

12. Ibid., 351.

13. Ibid., 350.

14. 469 F. Supp. 54 (N.D. Miss. 1978).

15. 614 F. Supp. 829 (S.D. Cal. 1985).

16. 283 F. Supp. 643 (S.D. N.Y. 1968).

17. For a more complete analysis of the *O'Melveny* case, see James F. Fotenos, *"FDIC v. O'Melveny & Myers*: Does Securities Counsel Owe to Investors and to Its Client a Duty to Conduct a Due Diligence Investigation of the Offering?" *Business Law News*, January 1993, 3.

CHAPTER ELEVEN: SICK OF LAWYERS — SICK OF THE LAW

1. See Anthony T. Kronman, *The Lost Lawyer* (Cambridge, Mass.: Belknap Press, 1993), part 1: Ideals.

2. Emily Barker, "Winston & Strawn Gets Ruthless," *American Lawyer*, June 1993, 72.

3. Susan Freinkel, "What Price Profits?" *American Lawyer*, June 1994, 59.

4. Ibid, 60, 62.

5. Ibid., 60.

6. D. M. Osborne, "Latham Sheds Its Skin," *American Lawyer*, June 1993, 62.

7. Barker, "Winston & Strawn Gets Ruthless," 70.

8. Tim O'Reiley, "K&S Sues a Spalding," *Fulton County Daily Report*, 21 July 1995, 1.

9. Karen Dillon, "The Death of a Career," *American Lawyer*, June 1994, 5, 70.

CHAPTER TWELVE: CHALLENGES FOR LAWYERS AND THE LEGAL PROFESSION

1. Statistics taken from an article by Paul Ciotti appearing in the *Los Angeles Times*, 25 August, 1988.

2. *Professionalism and the Bar: Program Materials* (Athens: Institute of Continuing Legal Education in Georgia, 1990), 6.

3. "ACCA survey shows most house counsel part of highest management circle," *Corporate Secretary – Corporate Directions*, 5 December, 1995, 185.

4. Private survey conducted by Kilpatrick & Cody in the summer of 1995.

5. Karen Dillon, "Brand Names at the Brink," *American Lawyer*, May 1995, 5.

6. John E. Morris, "Two Pioneers Make a Fixed-Fee Deal Work," *American Lawyer*, December 1993, 5.

7. Alison Frankel, "Debevoise Doesn't Budge," *American Lawyer*, June 1993, 76.

8. "The Am Law 100," *American Lawyer*, July/August 1995, supp. 55.

INDEX

Marketing: in 1960s, 12 – 13; in
1990s, 52 – 53; and
community service, 53 – 55.
See also Clients
Martindale count, 145
Maryland, poll of lawyers in,
83
Mediation, 96
Mergers, 122, 134; during 1960s,
24; during 1970s, 25
Meyerson, Harvey, 190
Miami, branch offices in, 203
Minority lawyers, 54, 198. *See
also* African American
lawyers; Women lawyers
Moise, Post & Gardner, 1, 2, 24

Negotiating styles, 128 – 34
Net operating loss (NOL), 122
New Jersey survey, 1990, 83
New York, 2; billable time in, 32,
82; starting salaries in, 62, 63,
65; profitability in, 69; and
higher compensation, 74;
reliance on practice model
of, 119 – 24; legal costs in,
123; prospects for partnership
in, 194 – 95; branch offices
in, 203
Ninth Circuit Court of Appeals,
170, 171, 174
North Carolina survey, 1990, 83

Offices, branch, 47, 203. *See also*
Technology, office
O'Melveny decision, 165, 170,
171 – 72, 174, 176
Opinions: publication of legal,
160, 161; unpublished, 175
Outsourcing, experimentation
with, 205
Overbilling, 97 – 98

Overstaffing, 106 – 8
Overwork, 81 – 85, 196 – 97. *See
also* Working conditions

Pagers, 58. *See also* Technology,
office
Paperwork, and relevant advice,
147
Paralegals, 48, 57
Partners: compensation of,
10 – 11, 65 – 72; as generalists,
14; managing, 30; hourly
rates of, 27; billing rates of,
33 – 34, 35; "nonequity,"
48; opportunity to become,
50, 194; African American,
55 – 56; women, 55 – 56;
supervision of associates by,
79; temporary, 85; senior,
86, 88, 193; personal liability
of, 88; big firm income of,
183; status of, 184 – 85;
reduction in profits per, 194;
specialization of, 195
Paul, Hastings, Janofsky &
Walker, 43
Philip Morris, 140
Piedmont Driving Club, 15
Posner, Richard, 169, 170
Pound, Roscoe, 160
Powell, Goldstein, Frazer &
Murphy, 1, 17, 21, 24, 25, 26,
47, 48
Price controls, and rate
schedules, 28
Productivity: increased, 113; and
compensation, 188. *See also*
Profitability
Profession: law as, 207 – 10;
status of legal, 191
Professionalism: loss of, 197;
Georgia's first convocation
on, 197 – 98

Made in the USA
Lexington, KY
20 December 2014